Abstract

During the past 30 years, Canadian craft has grown dramatically. However, public perception and mainstream academic study of craft have yet to catch up.

This multidisciplinary collection of 18 essays, presented at the symposium "Making and Metaphor: A Discussion of Meaning in Contemporary Craft," illustrates the complex and significant role of contemporary craft in society. The discipline of philosophy contributes both semiotics and feminism as tools for understanding craft. Historical analysis highlights how the fields of education, architecture and industrial design have influenced craft products and our perceptions of them. Social and cultural anthropology show how craft expresses gender and cultural identities, which are time-specific. And ethnology and museum studies reveal the assumptions involved in collecting, identifying and exhibiting craft.

This publication includes a keynote speech by broadcaster and writer Margaret Visser; an overview by Stephen Inglis, Director of Research at the Canadian Museum of Civilization; and commentary by Marjorie Halpin, Associate Professor of Anthropology and Curator of Ethnology at the University of British Columbia Museum of Anthropology.

Résumé

Au cours des trente dernières années, les métiers d'art canadiens ont pris un essor spectaculaire. Toutefois, les études théoriques et l'accueil du public accusent encore un certain retard.

Le présent recueil contient une collection de dix-huit essais qui ont été présentés sous forme de conférences à l'occasion du colloque interdisciplinaire Le faire et la métaphore – Un échange au sujet de la signification dans les métiers d'art contemporains. Ces essais illustrent le rôle complexe et important que jouent les métiers d'art contemporains dans la société. La philosophie met la sémiotique et le féminisme au service de l'interprétation des métiers d'art. L'analyse historique illustre comment les champs de l'éducation, de l'architecture et du dessin industriel influencent la production artistique et la façon dont elle est perçue. L'anthropologie sociale et culturelle met en lumière les particularités liées au sexe et à l'identité culturelle, qui sont le fruit d'une époque. Enfin, l'ethnologie et les études muséales prouvent des hypothèses qu'impliquent la collecte, l'identification et l'exposition d'œuvres.

La présente publication comprend un discours-programme de Margaret Visser, écrivaine et communicatrice, une vue d'ensemble des articles de Stephen Inglis, directeur de la Recherche au Musée canadien des civilisations et un commentaire de Marjorie Halpin, professeure agrégée d'anthropologie et conservatrice d'ethnologie au University of British Columbia Museum of Anthropology.

Making and Metaphor:
A Discussion of Meaning in
Contemporary Craft

Edited by Gloria A. Hickey

Canadian Centre for Folk Culture Studies
Mercury Series Paper 66

published by the
Canadian Museum of Civilization
with
The Institute for Contemporary Canadian Craft

CANADIAN CATALOGUING IN PUBLICATION DATA

Making and metaphor: a discussion of meaning
in contemporary craft

(Mercury series, ISSN 0316-1854)
(Paper/Canadian Centre for Folk Culture Studies,
ISSN 0316-1897; no. 66)
Includes some text and an abstract in French.
"Collection of eighteen essays that were presented at
the symposium Making and Metaphor: A Discussion
of Meaning in Contemporary Craft." – Abstract.
ISBN 0-660-14028-4

1. Arts and crafts movement – Canada –
    Congresses.
I. Hickey, Gloria, 1956-.
II. Canadian Museum of Civilization.
III. Canadian Centre for Folk Culture Studies.
IV. Title: A discussion of meaning
    in contemporary craft.
V. Series. VI. Series: Paper (Canadian Centre for
    Folk Culture Studies); no. 66.

NK841.H52 1994   745.5'0971   C94-980204-2

 **PRINTED IN CANADA**

Co-published by the

Canadian Museum of Civilization
100 Laurier Street
P.O. Box 3100, Station B
Hull, Quebec
J8X 4H2

and

**The Institute for
Contemporary Canadian Craft**

Cover photo: Diane Sullivan.
Detail from installation *Pillar to Pots*, 1992,
ceramic and floss.

Head of Production: Deborah Brownrigg.

Design: Harris Bhandari Design Associates.

The Institute for Contemporary Canadian Craft
is a non-profit educational organization registered
with Revenue Canada. It has a commitment to
further the understanding of the history, practice, and
value of the creative production of handmade objects
in Canada. It works as a think-tank on a project-to-
project basis and integrates these programs with the
activities of other craft-related organizations.

Canadä

OBJECT OF THE MERCURY SERIES

The Mercury Series is designed to permit the rapid
dissemination of information pertaining to the disciplines in which the Canadian Museum of Civilization
is active. Considered an important reference by the
scientific community, the Mercury Series comprises
over three hundred specialized publications on
Canada's history and prehistory.

Because of its specialized audience, the series consists
largely of monographs published in the language of
the author.

In the interest of making information available
quickly, normal production procedures have been
abbreviated. As a result, grammatical and typographi-
cal errors may occur. Your indulgence is requested.

Titles in the Mercury Series can be obtained by
writing to:

Mail Order Services
Canadian Museum of Civilization
100 Laurier Street
P.O. Box 3100, Station B
Hull, Quebec
J8X 4H2

BUT DE LA COLLECTION MERCURE

La collection Mercure vise à diffuser rapidement le
résultat de travaux dans les disciplines qui relèvent des
sphères d'activités du Musée canadien des civilisations. Considérée comme un apport important dans
la communauté scientifique, la collection Mercure
présente plus de trois cents publications spécialisées
portant sur l'héritage canadien préhistorique et
historique.

Comme la collection s'adresse à un public spécialisé,
celle-ci est constituée essentiellement de monogra-
phies publiées dans la langue des auteurs.

Pour assurer la prompte distribution des exemplaires
imprimés, les étapes de l'édition ont été abrégées. En
conséquence, certaines coquilles ou fautes de gram-
maire peuvent subsister : c'est pourquoi nous récla-
mons votre indulgence.

Vous pouvez vous procurer la liste des titres parus
dans la collection Mercure en écrivant au :

Service des commandes postales
Musée canadien des civilisations
100, rue Laurier
C.P. 3100, succursale B
Hull (Québec)
J8X 4H2

Table of Contents

Preface

Even though people involved in the arts almost always make distinctions between "art" and "craft," it is clear, as Howard Becker reminds us, that these terms refer to "ambiguous conglomerations of organizational and stylistic traits"[1] as well as social and political positions which are constantly in flux.

Museum collections provide one forum for bringing some of this ambiguity into focus through their practice of collection building, documentation and display, that is, the identification of object with time and place. Yet what many museums also seek today are living contextual links with the processes of making and using objects, links which can challenge and update conventional wisdom about collections and their significance.

This symposium, "Making and Metaphor: A Discussion of Meaning in Contemporary Craft," has provided an ideal opportunity for a wide range of professionals: makers, journalists, curators, and teachers to exchange views and share information. The site could not have been more appropriate, an institution dedicated to the work of craftspeople, from the Inuit hunters who fashioned the earliest decorated tools to today's heirs to the studio crafts movement.

The executive and committee members of the Institute for Contemporary Canadian Craft are to be congratulated for their hard work and foresight in organizing this symposium. The Canadian Museum of Civilization's contribution to the event and thus this publication would have been impossible without the hard work of Michael Ling.

Stephen Inglis
Director, Research Branch,
Canadian Museum of Civilization

1 Becker, H. *Art Worlds*, Berkeley: University of California Press, 1982, p. 273.

Préface

Bien que le monde des arts fasse presque toujours des distinctions entre l'art et l'artisanat, il semble évident, comme nous le rappelle Howard Becker, que ces mots évoquent des groupements ambigus de caractéristiques organisationnelles et stylistiques [1] aussi bien que des points de vue sociaux et politiques en évolution perpétuelle.

Les musées constituent un cadre favorable à la mise en lumière d'une facette de cette ambiguïté au moyen de la formation, de la documentation et de l'exposition des collections, c'est-à-dire par l'identification des objets dans le temps et l'espace. Mais à l'heure actuelle, beaucoup de musées cherchent également à découvrir les liens contextuels vivants entre les objets, leur fabrication et leur utilisation; ces liens susceptibles de contester et de remettre à jour le savoir traditionnel au sujet des collections et de leur signification.

Le symposium Le faire et la métaphore : Un échange au sujet de la signification dans les métiers d'art contemporains, a permis à un vaste échantillon de professionnels tels que les fabricants, les journalistes, les conservateurs de musée et les professeurs d'échanger leurs points de vue et de partager leurs connaissances. L'endroit ne pouvait mieux s'y prêter; une institution dédiée au travail des artisans, depuis les chasseurs Inuit qui ont façonné les plus anciens outils décorés jusqu'aux héritiers contemporains du mouvement de l'artisanat de commande.

Nous félicitons les membres de la direction et des comités de l'Institut pour les métiers d'art canadiens contemporains, pour leur travail acharné et leur prévoyance dans l'organisation de ce symposium. La participation du Musée canadien des civilisations à cet événement et par le fait même cette publication ont été rendues possible grâce aux efforts de Michael Ling.

Stephen Inglis
Director de la recherche,
Musée canadien des civilisations

1 Becker, H. *Art Worlds*, Berkeley: University of California Press, 1982, p. 273.

Introduction

The inaugural project of the Institute for Contemporary Canadian Craft was the interdisciplinary symposium "Making and Metaphor: A Discussion of Meaning in Contemporary Craft" held at the Canadian Museum of Civilization, in Hull, and the Canada Council Art Bank, in Ottawa, from October 22 to 24, 1993. At this forum, scholars, educators, writers, artists, and museum and gallery curators from across the country gathered to address a range of issues related to the development of contemporary craft and its place within the broader context of material culture.

The papers that were presented at the symposium and that make up this publication will fill a void in the information available to professionals in the field. Over the last thirty years, we have witnessed a spectacular growth in the production of craft in this country. Through the efforts of talented craftspeople, visionary gallery owners, hardworking craft associations, supportive government agencies, and enlightened benefactors, the handmade object has become a recognizable phenomenon of late-twentieth-century Canadian culture.

But perhaps because this has been largely a grass roots development, it has been overlooked by mainstream academics and museum curators. Today, a professional craftsperson working in Canada cannot readily point to a body of relevant, accessible scholarship that addresses her or his field. The implications for the education of crafts people, scholars, curators, writers, and, ultimately, the general public, are cause for concern.

It is hoped that these papers and the resulting passionate debate that took place among the 125 people who attended the symposium will be the beginning of a dialogue that will encourage increased scholarship related to craft practice, more informed curatorial approaches, and greater interest in building collections of contemporary Canadian work.

My appreciation is extended to Susan Warner Keene, Project Consultant, for her valuable contributions to the development of the symposium and journal. Her ideas and insights formed an important foundation for the project. Special thanks go to Gloria Hickey, who as editor has worked sensitively with the writers, copy editors, and translators, and with the Canadian Museum of Civilization (CMC) staff during the production of this volume. I am also grateful to Freya Godard and Johanne Plante, who copy-edited the English and French text respectively; translator Doris Drolet; proofreader Patricia Tolmie; and designer Sunil Bhandari. Throughout the project, the Institute's board of directors, committee members, and advisors have given invaluable advice and assistance.

The generosity of the Museum as our partner in this publication is greatly appreciated. Stephen Inglis, Director of Research, CMC, has provided counsel, encouragement, and energy that were integral to the realization of this project. The fact that these papers are presented as part of the Museum's important Mercury Series will provide the national and international network for contemporary craft research to reach a new and very wide audience involved in education. The efforts of Stephen, Deborah Brownrigg, Estelle Lauzon, and Madeleine Brazeau have made the publication possible.

And a heartfelt thanks is due to the writers of these essays whose interest in craft and its influence on our society is worthy of great consideration.

The alliances between organizations that have been developed during the planning of the Making and Metaphor project will be an important foundation for future projects. We hope that the dialogue that began over this weekend will lead to other projects meant to broaden the study of contemporary craft and its contributions to our cultural heritage.

Rosalyn J. Morrison
Executive Director
The Institute for Contemporary Canadian Craft

Introduction

Le projet inaugural de l'Institut pour les métiers d'art canadiens contemporains, le symposium interdisciplinaire intitulé Le faire et la métaphore : Un échange au sujet de la signification dans les métiers d'art contemporains, a eu lieu au Musée canadien des civilisations à Hull ainsi qu'à la Banque d'oeuvres d'art du Conseil des arts du Canada, à Ottawa, du 22 au 24 octobre 1993. À l'occasion de ce forum, érudits, éducateurs, écrivains, artistes et conservateurs de musée et de galerie de tous les coins du pays se sont réunis pour aborder une série de thèmes concernant l'évolution de l'artisanat contemporain et la place qu'il occupe au sein du contexte plus vaste de la culture matérielle.

Les exposés qui ont été présentés à ce symposium et qui forment le contenu de cette publication, répondront au besoin d'information éprouvé par les professionnels de ce domaine. Depuis trente ans, nous avons été les témoins d'une croissance spectaculaire de la production artisanale au pays. Grâce à l'effort soutenu des artisans de talent, des propriétaires de galerie d'art visionnaires, des associations d'artisanat dévouées, à l'appui des agences gouvernementales et des bienfaiteurs éclairés, l'objet fait à la main est devenu un phénomène identifiable de la culture canadienne de la fin du vingtième siècle.

Cette évolution n'a pas attiré l'attention des universitaires et des conservateurs de musée établis, peut-être à cause de sa nature largement populaire. Un artisan professionnel oeuvrant au Canada aujourd'hui ne peut spontanément se référer à un savoir scientifique pertinent et accessible qui s'adresse à son domaine. Les conséquences de cet état de choses sur l'éducation des artisans, les érudits, les conservateurs de musée, les écrivains et, finalement, le grand public, sont préoccupantes.

Nous espérons que ces exposés et le débat passionnant auquel ils ont donné lieu parmi les 125 personnes présentes au symposium, constitueront le début d'un dialogue favorable à un savoir scientifique accru relié à la pratique de l'artisanat, à des approches de conservation plus éclairées et à un intérêt grandissant dans la formation de collections d'oeuvres canadiennes contemporaines.

Nous aimerions sincèrement remercier les auteurs de ces exposés dont l'intérêt pour l'artisanat et son influence sur notre société a un très grand mérite.

Rosalyn J. Morrison
Directeur exécutif
L'Institut pour les métiers d'art canadiens contemporains

Acknowledgements

We gratefully acknowledge the generous financial support for this publication from the Government of Canada through the Department of Canadian Heritage and the Secretary of State and the Canada Council Jean A. Chalmers Fund for the Crafts; from the Government of Ontario through the Ministry of Culture, Tourism and Recreation; from the Sheila Hugh Mackay Foundation, Imperial Oil Limited, The Massey Foundation, le Musée des arts décoratifs de Montréal, and the Toronto-Dominion Bank; and from Howard Collinson, Harriet Lewis, William (Grit) Laskin, Marie Sauvé Lloyd, Dorothy Burnham, Rachelle Geneau, Walter Ostrom, Diana Reitberger, Katherine Vansittart, Jeannot Blackburn, Léopold Foulem, Paul Mathieu, and Richard Milette.

Our thanks are also extended to the following organizations and individuals for their contributions to this project:

Arthur Andersen & CO., SC

The Canada Council Art Bank

Canadian Anthropology Society

Canadian Bookbinders and Book Artists Guild

Canadian Clay and Glass Gallery

Canadian Federation of Friends of Museums

Canadian Museum of Civilization

Canadian Museums Association

The Craft Studio at Harbourfront Centre

Fusion: The Ontario Clay and Glass Association

The George R. Gardiner Museum of Ceramic Art/
    Royal Ontario Museum

Harris Bhandari Design Associates

Ian Gray & Associates Limited

Musée des arts décoratifs de Montréal

The Museum for Textiles

National Gallery of Canada

Ontario Arts Council

Ontario Association of Art Galleries

Ontario Crafts Council

Prime Gallery

Professional Art Dealers Association of Canada

Sheridan College School of Crafts and Design

University of British Columbia Museum of Anthropology

University of Waterloo

Margaret Visser

Keynote: The Language of Things

Margaret Visser teaches Classics at York University in Toronto. She also lectures and broadcasts internationally, and has been the recipient of several awards for her books, which include Much Depends on Dinner.

Discours-programme : Le langage des choses

Faisant partie d'un peuple moderne, nous avons une vision idéale de nous-mêmes comme des individus créatifs, uniques et résolus à nous découvrir et à nous exprimer le plus authentiquement possible. Paradoxalement, la société qui engendre ce même individualisme finit par réduire l'importance de l'individu ou par rendre l'individualisme destructeur à cause d'un matérialisme excessif. Des objets fabriqués à la chaîne, normalisés et vendus en boutique étouffent non seulement nos villes mais aussi notre esprit et notre imagination; ils aménuisent les possibilités d'exprimer qui nous sommes. L'ambivalence ressentie face aux triomphes technologiques n'est donc pas étonnante de même que la demande perpétuelle pour des objets fabriqués à la main, chacun d'entre eux entièrement façonné par une personne à partir de la réalisation d'une vision personnelle, au moyen de compétences et de talents durement acquis et cultivés.

En créant des objets de nos propres mains, tout en dépassant largement l'usage auquel ils sont destinés, nous mettons effectivement en pratique cet individualisme que nous admirons tant et avec raison, mais d'une manière qui enrichira et embellira le monde et sans nuire à quiconque par ce geste.

The word "craft" originally meant "cunning power" – skill, strength, and intelligence all rolled into one. *A* craft – embroidery for example, or wood-work, or weaving – was also a cunning power: a specific area of expertise. Not possessing the power oneself, and needing it, meant one had to bow to it, pay for it, accept its mystique in the people who had earned the capability required. So potent and revered were craftsmen that in many mythological traditions the earth itself, as well as humankind, was created by a divine craftsman, very often compared to a potter, shaping creation from formless matter. Even the Old Testament has God modelling the first human creature out of clay, and then breathing life into it.

Expertise, however, can be used for good or for ill, and people who had mastered a craft, a thing of great power, could be experienced not only as necessary and admirable, but also as threatening and dangerous. "Craft" was associated with exclusive and secretive guilds and brotherhoods. And "crafty," of course, is "clever," with a special deviousness and malignancy.

How different is the usage of the word "craft" in a modern phrase like "arts and crafts" or in a word like "handicrafts"! ("Handi" sounds like a put-down right there – like a child's word. And indeed many people nowadays seem to think of "crafts" as an amusement for primary-school children, when it is not a therapeutic device or a harmless activity to while away the time.) The word "crafts" has come to be used for hobbies, *outlets* for cre-ativity. And crafts that are not done for money are by that very token, in the modern world, activities not to be taken seriously. Such crafts are practiced in merely *free* (that is not working, and not paid) time – unless they are per-formed by simple folk who make "folk art" souvenirs for us to buy when we are on holiday: handicrafts are often sold as mementos of exotic places, past times, and ways of living that are assuredly dying.

Where "craft" is used to denote skill expended on things handmade for normal, everyday use, the connotation can still be patronizing, for "art" (a term unquestionably of praise) has been reserved since the nineteenth cen-tury for things, chiefly painting and sculpture, made, not to be used, but only contemplated for their beauty; it also became a term for the skill required to make them.

Now in spite of such condescending and barely examined attitudes, there is substantial interest in the crafts in modern society. I want to suggest a few of the reasons – both good and questionable – for this. We might as well begin with the fact that the things craftsmen make used to be available only from craftsmen, but these days machines supply us with serviceable versions of most of them. If "art" is essentially useless and all the more admirable for that (allowing one to concentrate without distraction on beauty), then "craft," in becoming strictly speaking unnecessary, has acquired a goodly lease of respect: it is regarded as far more "artistic" than it used to be.

From a purely financial point of view, machine-made goods, after all, are what is cheap these days: cups and saucers, chairs, clothes, books and vehicles – all are machine-made, mass-produced, standardized, ubiquitous. Having your clothes made by hand, or your books especially bound, is now regarded as proof that you are rich. It might also be thought to constitute proof that you have taste: a person with a real wool carpet on the floor is a notch up from someone with mere nylon; and a real wool *handknotted* carpet lifts you onto an altogether higher plane. For crafting goods takes time (to say nothing of artistry), and time costs money.

Even if you weave your own cloth or make your own bread, you have to have the time to do so and be sufficiently privileged – knowing how to go about learning and having the time – to learn the skills required. Handcrafted objects prove either that you can buy what few can afford or that you have the time (that is, the money) to make things for the pleasure of making them. Or you have been able to afford to travel where people still habitually make things by hand or where they make them for tourists to buy – and such places are definitively elsewhere; it again presupposes money to get there from here. Or you have inherited old things made by means of vanished skills; these heirlooms will be valuable and worth more and more (because they will become rarer and rarer) as time goes on.

But the chicness of the new can almost rival in prestige the patina of age. *Everybody,* these days, can have a set of stainless steel dinnerware, but only the few can eat with – and thereby impress their guests with – streamlined, designer, one-off forks with somebody's signature on them, proving that they are entirely the chic thing to have. They are *not* what everybody can have – not even, indeed, what everybody would *want* to have. (Exclusivity can rejoice in shutting out the uncomprehending as well as the simply unable.) Modern design has achieved a high degree of confidence, now that it can glory in the status that is conferred when an object is deemed, by the present arbiters of taste, to be "on the cutting edge."

This rather disagreeable way of looking at things takes its stand of course within the system, within modernity. To say these things and live by them is to have "bought" (to use a modern expression) the conveniences of modern life – where a smashed glass is barely worth bothering about except for the nuisance of having to sweep away the pieces, where suits are bought in half an hour "off the hook," where socks are thrown away if they develop holes. I've just been researching the history of the chest of drawers and have found that this piece of furniture became common only in the nineteenth century, in the middle classes. What had happened was that people started owning vast amounts of stuff. It was no longer reasonable to keep it all in a wooden box that you had to empty every time you wanted to get something out of the bottom. Now you needed *separate drawers* – a whole series of stacked chests in fact – for socks, underwear, sweaters, pants, and a "bottom drawer" for the junk you didn't need, but which accumulated relentlessly anyway, and thank God for somewhere to put it all, out of sight. We now have lots of possessions, and none of them is particularly special. We rarely expect them to last or to be irreplaceable – and next year the clothes at least will be out of fashion anyway.

In a world like this – I don't have to go on giving examples, we all know it intimately, you cannot avoid its clutches – crafts continue to exert power, in spite of the cramped and demeaning place to which modernity constantly tries to relegate them. That strength, however – in German, *Kraft* – needs redefining if we are to understand how it fits into the present social and economic structure. Handmade objects exist now always *in dialogue* with machine-made things; they speak to us necessarily in the modern idiom. They respond to the world of factories, comment upon the modern condition. It is possible to argue that they exist not only *in spite of* modernity but, in their present role, *because of* it.

Craft objects can fill in, compensate for, what machine-made products cannot provide. For example, hand-crafted objects are *personal*. We, in the modern world, are used to paying a higher price for things, even services, that are "personalized." The word itself is instructive: it is a new verb for a new need, thus making us feel that personhood is being restored. The word was not needed in the past because the personal imbued everything: it had not been stripped away. Nowadays we pay extra for something with a signature on it – couture clothes, hand knitting, a restaurant where waiters watch your every move, filling your wineglass before you know you need more, even going so far as to spread your napkin on your lap! An object means more still if you know who made it, if you sleep under a quilt crafted by your great-aunt rather than something from, say, Consumers Distributing.

Notice the words "rather than": modern people use handmade things, if they can afford them, *by choice*. The alternative is now the easier one, the one more obvious as well as cheaper. But we choose what is harder and "dearer" – dearer in both senses: more expensive and more lovable. What this tells us is that modernity has sacrificed the personal for the convenient but that it often, though paradoxically, regrets the decision.

Modernity also prefers ease to meaning: to care for an object because you know who made it, when, and for whom, is essentially an unmodern emotion, an endowing of an object with a value that lies beyond money. Modern critical analysts would call that mystification. We can see what they call mystification clearly institutionalized and made into a tradition, in the Japanese art of raku pottery. A beautiful raku tea bowl is a simple, irregular object, as much like something found in nature as is compatible with its intentionally functional purpose. You rejoice in the imperfections, love the bumps, wobbles, and cracks. You use the object with appreciation, with intensity, even with fervor, admiring it, balancing it in your hands, noting the comfort with which you sip tea from its lip. A really good raku piece is given a name. Nowadays its maker too is known. In the past it was the owners of raku cups who used to be documented, as a sort of pedigree. A person who owns a famous tea bowl (I remind you that the cup *in itself* is utterly simple) is allotted a special place at *Chanoyu,* the tea ceremony. Value *is added* to such a cup, and more and more meaning accrues to it the longer it remains in use. Eventually the cup becomes almost a test, a touchstone of the beholder's taste and ability to appreciate the beautiful. (If you can't see the beauty in it, you are judged unacceptably insensitive.)

All this sort of thing has been greatly played down – shall we say given up? – by modern mass production techniques, by egalitarianism, by the choice we made as a culture to prefer replaceability to uniqueness and to make everything available to all even if it means that nothing shall be special. To make objects by hand deliberately and to seek out and prefer handmade objects is a response to sameness and universal availability; it reintroduces, at least in one corner of our lives, a whole possibility of seeing and feeling that modernity works hard to negate. Age undoubtedly adds value to a raku cup. We too feel that old is special, above all if the skills expressed in an old and beautiful thing are skills that no longer exist. We pay money for what is rare: it is the homage modernity pays to what it tries to discourage!

The modern talent for abstraction, the ability to stand apart from ourselves and watch and analyse ourselves, causes modern craftsmen to question the way things are. Many artists feel compelled to create objects that parody themselves, that mock the materials out of which they are made, or that implicitly criticize the values of the very culture from which they spring. Among the most amusing of modern craftsmanly inventions are body ornaments made in materials that actually make fun of expensive, rare jewellery: cork necklaces for example, or earrings that are blatantly made of plastic or of curtain-tassels. Here craft joins hands with modernity's commitment to making everything available to all. Anyone (ostensibly at any rate) could afford this jewellery – provided that the designer is not too famous, in which case the name can add greatly to the price. It also means that jewellery can be *large,* and that neatly fits modern requirements: we have little time for intimacy these days, and if we are to make an impression on other people we need to make it *fast.* It is as though we were billboards flashing past speeding cars: the message has to be loud and large. There is daring, humour, and restraint in this new trend – but also an excess that is born of pressures specific to modern life.

The crafts allow professional artists a realm for wit and for play. Intense creativity often finds powerful release in the crafts, where new materials are tried and things made that prolong the childhood in all of us: fantastic cupboards, strange (because essentially frivolous) designs for desks, unexpected forms for lighting fixtures. Because craft (as opposed to fine art) is spent on things that are of use, craft objects inspire playfulness. They bring delight and imagination into a world dominated by mechanical, rational standardizations of many kinds. There is always a stern limit built into successful objects of use, however: they have to be functional, comfortable, and recognizable to some extent, no matter how outrageously original they look: they have to do their job. But then, restraint, categorizations, and rules make up an essential aspect of both playfulness and wit.

Playfulness in the crafts is often expressed in the mixing of media or of creative genres (mixing thrown pottery with modelled for example) or creating hybrid styles. Traditions are quoted from and reinterpreted. In the course of seemingly innocent play, we feel free to borrow everything, from Navajo rug designs to Maori carving forms. This eclecticism is of course very up-to-date; it is multicultural, a result of the communications systems created by modernity. Our modern condition of being in touch with all the possibilities at once thus provides us with a great many new ideas. The down side is that such borrowing is all very self-conscious – it cannot be otherwise. We don't *believe* in these styles, and never intend to adopt the world view they express. We merely *explore* them.

We have to admit to something sinister about this, something almost imperialistic about treating the world – in this instance other people's artistic style – as so conveniently "our oyster." We have to be extremely careful, respectful, aware of what we are doing, and above all able to integrate newly derived ideas into our own honest and original vision. Otherwise, there can be something uncomfortably tasteless about revelling in styles created by cultures that are dying before our eyes, dying in large part because our own culture is so pervasive, being backed by the prestige precisely of the modern.

Modern crafts often express modern concerns about ecology. The insistence on using ordinary, non-exotic woods for furniture might be significant here, and also the anti-mechanistic choice of forms that are rough and nubbly, that seem to us more "natural." Often craft objects emphasize the nature of their materials and deliberately attempt, like raku pottery, to revel in what emerges when nature is moulded – leaving it, within bounds applied as loosely as possible, to take its course. There is an *accepting* attitude here, one which can be intended and read as a direct criticism of the merciless and short-sighted control that our technology and our science so often seek to impose on the world. To be able to control the production of an object, but to decide freely to let nature be a participant in that creation is an almost ritual expression of respect. It can represent a rejection of the very human desire, which has in modern times become a real and dangerous option, to change nature (often, alas, permanently) in order to suit our own short-term, highly culture-specific convenience. The incorporation of "found" objects into art is often, I believe, evidence of a more appreciative and accepting attitude to life. It can also constitute a sharp criticism of the waste and ugliness of the litter and refuse that issue from a factory-centred universe.

In that universe we all mostly live, now. Its advantages are very obvious: few of us present do not own a mass-produced car, or do without ready-made clothes, or disdain factory-made pots, pans, or bathroom equipment. But because we are modern people, all of us have an ideal vision of ourselves as individuals, creative, unique, determined to find and express our truest selves. Ironically enough, the society that produced that very individualism in fact ends up, through its material excess, demeaning the individual or turning individualism into something destructive. Mass-produced, standard-ized, shop-bought objects not only clog our cities but muffle our minds and imaginations; they flatten out the possibilities of self-expression. In spite of the ads emphasizing endless novelty and inventiveness, living with a constant stream of these objects actually crushes real variety and difference. It is no wonder then that there is an ambivalence towards the triumphs of technol-ogy and an indestructible demand for handmade things, each of them entire-ly crafted by one person out of an achieved personal vision, and by means of skills and gifts painstakingly earned and cultivated.

Making something with your hands goes beyond the merely rational, and we are also becoming wary about living all in our heads. We have learned that our famous modern individualism can in fact be narcissistic, greedy, unheeding of other people's needs. In making things by hand, firmly going beyond necessity to do so, we are in fact practising the individualism we so much and so rightly admire, but in a manner that will actually add to the rich-ness and beauty in the world without harming anybody else in the process.

Stephen Inglis

Overview: Forming Discourse

Stephen Inglis is Director of the Research

Branch at the Canadian Museum of Civilization.

He has specialized in the study of

Canadian artists and their communities.

De la formation de courants de pensée

Depuis l'ouverture du Musée canadien des civilisations en 1989 et jusqu'à tout récemment, le sex-shop qui avait pignon sur rue en face du Musée a été le théâtre d'une vive controverse. Le propriétaire a en effet mené une longue lutte contre la ville de Hull qui voulait l'exproprier et remplacer son commerce par un autre plus «convenable» dans l'environnement d'un nouveau musée national. Tour à tour, les politiciens municipaux et les promoteurs de tourisme de la Commission de la capitale nationale ont crié au scandale devant l'étalage des «objets de plaisir» et autres dessous affriolants qui, selon eux, déparaient l'architecture du Musée. En dernier ressort, le propriétaire a présenté une demande d'exemption à titre d'«institution culturelle» et menacé d'ouvrir le deuxième étage. Il a finalement plié bagage.

Le local est maintenant occupé par la boutique Hors-Série gérée par le Conseil des artistes en métiers d'art de l'Outaouais. On aurait tort, à mon avis, de conclure au triomphe de l'artisanat sur le sexe. J'y vois plutôt un échange de lieux d'expression de deux traits fondamentaux de la société humaine. Le rôle ambigu des métiers d'art a suscité divers courants de pensée, comme en témoignent les comptes rendus des périodiques, les catalogues et les conférences.

Le premier de ces courants voit dans les métiers d'art la fabrication d'objets et s'attache donc principalement au produit et à son statut. Il tient essentiellement en une polémique au sujet de l'ostracisme qui sous-tend la pratique de l'art moderne, les théoriciens modernistes et certains postmodernistes excluant toujours de l'art les ouvrages d'artisanat.

Le deuxième courant insiste sur l'artisanat en tant que procédé ou, si l'on veut, sur la représentation concrète plutôt que métaphorique de l'évolution des mœurs. Il s'attache à la nature même des peuples, à la société, aux lieux, à la relation avec la collectivité, au «sentiment d'appartenance» et, dans ce sens, va beaucoup plus loin et est moins focalisé.

Le troisième courant voit dans les métiers d'art une tradition humaine au sens le plus large. Le discours emprunte à l'anthropologie, à la culture matérielle, à l'histoire de l'art et à la philosophie. Tous ces domaines sont propices à un dialogue entre praticiens et commentateurs, comme celui que veut susciter la présente conférence.

La diversité et la qualité formatrice des divers courants de pensée sur les métiers d'art révèlent sans doute une réticence fondamentale à parler du concret. La société semble avoir toujours craint ce qui prête à plus d'une interprétation : l'art et l'artisanat, la sculpture et la peinture, le masculin et le féminin (Ellison, 1993), aussi bien que les déclarations les plus récentes des médias pour initiés.

A small but poignant drama was played out across the street from the Canadian Museum of Civilization from the time the new building opened in 1989 until just a few months ago. The sex shop located there became engaged in a protracted battle with the City of Hull, which wanted to expropriate the business for what it felt was a more appropriate neighbour for a new national museum. A succession of upstanding Hull city politicians and National Capital Commission tourism promoters weighed in with outrage that the curves of the museum's architecture were being undercut by a display of pleasure aids and fancy underwear. When every other argument was exhausted, the shop owner claimed an exemption as a "cultural institution" and threatened to expand to the second floor. In the end, he moved.

The space is now occupied by a craft gallery named Hors-Série, the retail outlet of a craft council, the Conseil des artistes en métiers d'art de l'Outaouais. That might be misread, in a forum such as this, as a triumph of the crafts over sex. I would suggest that it is rather an exchange of venue by two essential features of human society, both of which are under a certain amount of pressure in the late twentieth century. This pressure accounts, at least in part, for the diverse range of ways of talking and writing about the crafts, as is evident in journals, catalogues, and conferences.

The first of these is the discourse on craft as object, a discussion mainly concerned with products and their status. This discourse takes the form largely of a debate with modernist art's apparent practice of excluding craft, since modernist and much post-modernist art theory continues to exclude work in craft materials.

One of the strengths of this discourse is that it brings a greater precision and sophistication to the language of craft since it adopts accepted terms for discussing form, colour, and metaphor. In addition, this discourse continues to challenge the conventions concerning the status and boundaries of works of art. Yet the discussion is intrinsically exclusionist from the point of view of wider craft practice, because it is predicated on the object's being treated like painting or sculpture and because only a tiny elite of this work could qualify. It rests on the "foot in the door" aspiration which must become the quickly closed door to avoid all the embarrassing stuff that might trail behind, that is, craft work which doesn't meet the criteria for the expressive object.

A second form of discourse is directed towards craft as process. This form is more concerned with the *making* than the *metaphor,* with craft as an evolving attitude towards living. It focuses on the nature of people, the society, the site, the relationship to community, and "a sense of place" and is, as such, far broader and less focused. This discourse is more concerned with social satisfaction than comparative success and remains the main form of communication between practitioners. Credit must be given here to the "society within a society" described by Lucie-Smith (1981), which has generated this discourse and is at least partly responsible for the survival of many crafts in this century.

A third form of discourse centres on craft as a broader human tradition. This uses some of the languages of anthropology, material culture, art history, and philosophy. All these fields are moving toward the dialogue between practitioners and commentators, such as the one to which this conference aspires. This form can be divided into two complementary branches. One is mainly concerned with the local and the recent, for example, the history of studio crafts in Canada. There has been a slow but steady growth in collection building and context building through the integration of crafts with the social movements of design and other arts. Links have been established with British, French, and American movements as well as with popular culture. The study of the studio crafts movement has now reached a point where it has yielded some promising results.

Yet another branch of the wider discourse deals with crafts internationally and throughout history. It is comparative and cross-cultural and refers to periods in which all art was craft, or where it is still seen as such. Much continues to be "leavened in" to the craft discourse from the immense body of knowledge and practice in the arts. Writers such as Robert Hughes (1993) have recognized craft traditions as legitimate and dynamic counterpoints to the humourlessness and ugliness of much contemporary art. Yet some of this information challenges many cherished notions of craft discourse, such as the faith that craftspeople will by "nature" (that is, by culture) eventually become fully integrated, respected members of society, like "lawyers with looms." Developed, if not initiated, by utopians like Morris and Ruskin, this line of opinion proposes that in earlier periods of European history – and in other parts of the world down to this day where the crafts retain their functional prerogatives – makers were highly respected by their communities, and it was only with the industrial age that the skills and roles to which today's makers are heir took a great fall in status.

There is very little in either the history of European craftsmanship or in the ethnography of village or rural makers to support this view. Although the work of these specialists is *essential* to society, their actual social role is almost always ambiguous. While we might expect most people to be suspicious of an artist who hurls paint and cigarette butts at a canvas, we might be surprised at the more ancient, profound, and persistent suspicion of a person who can make perfect, complex joints in wood, an exquisite jewelled diadem, or a marvel of precisely woven colour and texture.

In fact, makers in most societies are considered by others to be practising mysteries. Special knowledge and skill is always somewhat threatening to those that don't possess it, and artists have always had to find unusual ways of defending and maintaining themselves, for example, by developing exclusive dialects of language, as we're doing here. Ambiguity and a deep involvement with ritual have been some ways in which craftsmen have traditionally countered the power of landowners and rulers. Ultimately, ambiguity embodies a certain kind of social power, and makers have traditionally emphasized this characteristic in opposition to social norms.

It is my contention that similar attitudes and prejudices continue to colour the relationships between creative people, particularly those who employ traditional craft skills, and the general public. Although this is not my call to more mystical or ritual activity among makers, nor an elaborate rationale for why most people will never really understand what they do, it is useful, I believe, to consider the social conditions under which this work will always be carried out, that is, somewhat on the side, somewhat at odds, somewhat, by its nature, both fascinating and disturbing to others. That both makers and critics constantly refer to "ambiguity," "subtlety," and "illusion" and even appeal to the unconscious indicates to me that some of the intrinsic qualities of craftsmanship rest in things that are difficult to express in concrete or conventional terms (see for example Duffy 1989). It is probably *those* characteristics that have enabled these ancient and precious forms of expression to survive technological change and artistic marginality to emerge lean, but still with powerful aspirations.

The diversity and formative quality of the various types of discourse on craft probably reveal a fundamental reluctance to talk about making. There seems to have always existed a fear by society of objects that can mean more than one thing at once: art and craft, sculpture and painting, masculine and feminine (Ellison 1993), and the most contemporary statements in the most arcane media.

References

Duffy, Helen. 1989. "Introductory Essay." In *Directions: From Historical Sources*. Toronto: Museum for Textiles, 5-6.

Ellison, Robert A. 1993. "Judgment Call: The 29th Ceramic National." *American Craft,* October/November: 46-51.

Hughes, Robert. 1993. *The Culture of Complaint*. New York: Oxford University Press.

Lucie-Smith, Edward. 1981. *The Story of Craft: The Craftsman's Role in Society*. Ithaca, N.Y.: Cornell University Press.

Towards a Language of Craft

PaulMathieuMichelParadisMicheleHardyKathyM'Closkey

Paul Mathieu

The Space of Pottery:

An Investigation of the Nature of Craft

Paul Mathieu is an internationally exhibited
Montreal potter who received his MFA from the
University of California in Los Angeles.

L'espace de la poterie

Une présentation d'une demi-heure illustrée de diapositives sur la nature particulière des recherches spatiales appliquées à la poterie et par extension à la céramique et à d'autres pratiques artisanales. La source première de cette présentation est une conférence par Michel Foucault intitulée «des espaces autres» qui adresse certaines caractéristiques de l'espace.

En établissant les différences et les relations entre les utopies (art) et ce qu'il nomme les hétérotopies, «les espaces autres» (artisanat), cette présentation propose d'analyser et de comprendre l'artisanat en dehors des polarités et dichotomies du débat art/artisanat. Lors de la présentation, les qualités et caractéristiques de certains espaces quant à leur universalité, leur relation au temps, au rituel et à la juxtaposition ainsi que la difficulté de tenir un discours théorique sur ces espaces seront explorés. Les diapositives (±50) utilisées pour illustrer le texte sont très diverses et leur variété couvre des exemples d'artisanat contemporain (surtout canadiens) ainsi que des exemples historiques dans d'autres disciplines (peinture, sculpture, tissus).

This paper, which was presented in French at the symposium, is published here in English at the author's request.

Cette présentation adresse plusieurs des thèmes suggérés : le rôle de la fonction, le matériau comme signifiant, un modèle pour l'appréciation esthétique, le rôle de l'individu créateur, etc. Le but de cette présentation n'est pas de proposer un modèle fixe pour comprendre l'artisanat mais de présenter, d'examiner et d'analyser certaines caractéristiques propres aux pratiques artisanales dans l'espoir de générer un débat sur ces problèmes.

First, I would like to thank Leopold Foulem for reading this paper, as well as the Institute for Contemporary Canadian Crafts for inviting me to speak at this symposium. I will take a few minutes extra in order to make a few political statements; I rarely have the opportunity to do so.

I feel honoured to be able to present my ideas here at the Canadian Museum of Civilization, an institution that wouldn't have an example of my work in its collection because what I do isn't traditional enough. What tradition, may I ask?

I am a potter, and what I do is craft; I have no problem with those words, which belong to a long history that has no reason to envy any other craft or art, even now. Just as the gay community has appropriated the term "queer," so is it time for us to celebrate anew certain terms that define what we do.

If you go across the river to the National Gallery, you see numerous examples of historical crafts, in metal-smithing most notably. When I go to such places, I feel that I am not welcome, that I do not belong there since what I do isn't welcome. Why are historical crafts acceptable and contemporary crafts almost totally rejected and ignored? I wonder if I'll have to wait another hundred years like Morris and de Morgan before what I do belongs there. How many curators from the National Gallery are present here today? Why is that? Why is craft ignored? That is the question I will partly answer today.

At a symposium held by the Craft Association of British Columbia in November 1991, Doris Shadbolt (1992) also proposed an answer. She said, "Craft is about the very qualities that current art [theory] denies ... the theory-dominated cerebral climate which dominates today's art will change sooner or later and then there will be a powerful expression of reactive response. And a reaffirmation of the importance of the crafts will be at the centre of that response."

I applaud such far-sightedness, yet wish she had preached by example too and had included a few pieces of Emily Carr's pottery in the retrospective she had organized for the National Gallery a few years before. Actions speak louder than words.

The art world is singularly ignorant of craft. It knows only two ways to deal with it: one is assimilation, by addressing its manifestations only when they look and act like conventional art; the other is ghettoization, by ignoring it completely. This ghettoization is in effect censorship.

Another problem is the obsession of art with categories. Despite recent talk of de-hierarchization, the crossing of borders, and openness to difference and otherness, the prevalent categories and taxonomies are still effective. Well, crafts are unclassifiable. They defy categories. In fact, craft is the activity where de-hierarchization, the crossing of borders and categories, and differences between the races and sexes are explored the most thoroughly today, as well as historically. The one border the art world refuses to cross is that of craft. What exactly is it afraid of?

Craft has always been inherently political, open to change, and aware of contemporaneity; it still is.

What is a potter doing meddling with theory and ideas, anyway? I believe it is essential to confront the art world in the language it speaks, to address the problem on *its* territory. We must all work together: that is where the work is to be done.

The ideas I want to discuss here come from many sources but especially from two articles I read recently. The first is the "Comment" by the Toronto art critic John Bentley Mays (1985) in *American Craft*. In this article, Mays justifies his reasons for ignoring crafts, "not because craft or craft-as-art (as I have experienced it) are inferior to art, but because they are NOT art." This kind of commentary truly irritates me because it is too easy simply to state that craft is not art without explaining its true nature. It is lazy as well as fraudulent. The other source of inspiration for me was a lecture given by the French thinker Michel Foucault (1986) in 1967. This lecture, entitled "Of Other Spaces," analyses certain characteristics of contemporary space. Hence these reflections on "the space of pottery."

The element common to all art forms is space. But the different ways that different art forms deal with space is what sets them apart from one another.

What then is the space of pottery? I am talking here of pottery in its most simple, essential form, for example, an ordinary white teapot (see Figure 1). But by "pot" I do not mean simply an object for containment but basically any form dealing somehow with the principle of containment or the articulation of a movable volumetric space through its generative process. I am thinking of the work of Ruth McKinley but also of Viola Frey's large figures or Richard Milette's vessel of 1990. In my opinion, most ceramic "sculptures" are as much pots as anything else, since they are generated by volume rather than mass, a characteristic essential to pottery. A Rodin bronze is also hollow, but the form has been generated by mass. The void inside a Rodin is empty. It is not significant. On the other hand, the space inside the Viola Frey is pregnant and formally, conceptually relevant because that void articulates the form. It is not empty but on the contrary, full, meaningful, significant, like the air under pressure in a balloon. The word "volume" makes me think of its other meaning, a book, which is also an object that contains, transports, preserves, and transmits knowledge, all of which are activities intrinsic also in pottery.

There has recently been a profusion of writings that emphasize the relation of pottery to painting and sculpture, and many ceramists have taken the same position in the making of their work. We have seen Peter Voulkos's plates referred to as "drawings" and some pots labelled "still life." This semantic ambiguity is on the whole legitimate and certainly legitimized by the marketplace, but it is my intention here to establish how pottery is *different* and to bring some understanding of its nature, not only the nature of the objects themselves, but also that of the practice and discipline as a whole.

Michel Foucault was an influential thinker, particularly interested in the relationship between power and knowledge. He investigated "otherness," that is, the mental institution, the prison, and until his death from AIDS a few years ago, sexuality. Foucault's premise is that the notion of space is central to our time and that "our life is still governed by a certain number of oppositions that remain inviolable that our institutions and practices have not yet dared to break down." As examples, he lists private space versus public space, leisure space versus work space, and, what is most important here, cultural space versus useful space. This last category includes the now famous debate about art versus craft.

In this category of cultural as opposed to useful spaces, he is interested in spaces "that are in relation to all other sites, while they contradict all other sites." These spaces are of two main types. The first he calls "utopias," which are not real spaces, but basically unreal spaces (a category including the objects our culture usually refers to as works of art); the other he calls "heterotopias" (or other spaces), which are real spaces where "all the other real sites that are to be found within a culture are simultaneously represented, contested and inverted." These "other spaces" follow five basic principles.

The first principle is that all cultures create "other spaces": they are universal. These other spaces are "privileged, sacred spaces reserved for specific purposes." They are of two main types: crisis heterotopias like hospitals, boarding schools, or the motel for the honeymoon; and deviation heterotopias such as psychiatric hospitals, prisons, or retirement homes.

The second principle of heterotopias is that their function is determined by context and that it changes with time and culture. His example is the cemetery because although all cultures have places that serve the purpose of cemeteries, this function is different in each culture and also changes as the culture changes.

The third principle is that heterotopias juxtapose, in a single place, several sites that are in themselves incompatible. The theatre and cinema are perfect examples: in a real room, a seemingly three-dimensional image is projected onto a flat screen, and the action may take place in another place, another time, another world. Shopping centres and gardens are also in this category since they bring together objects and species from all over the world, and so do carpets when they are representations of gardens that can be moved in space.

The fourth principle is that heterotopias are linked to slices of time, either in its accumulation, like museums or libraries, or its transitoriness like fairgrounds or holiday resorts. In our culture, fairgrounds have also become permanent. Disneyland is a good example.

The fifth principle is that heterotopias command certain rituals: "they suppose a system of opening and closing that both isolates them and makes them penetrable." For example, baths or saunas in certain cultures demand a certain ritual in order to gain entrance, cinemas and theatres require tickets and reservations, the prison requires culpability for crime.

Now, the function of these "other spaces" is to create "a space that is other, another real space as perfect, meticulous, and as well arranged as ours is messy, ill constructed, and jumbled." Mirrors are both utopias and heterotopias, since they show real spaces in an unreal space, but, according to Foucault, the ship is the heterotopia *par excellence,* "a floating piece of space, a place without a place, that exists by itself, that is closed in on itself and at the same time is given over to the infinity of the sea."

Well, ships are vessels, and so are pots, since both are meant not only to hold and contain, but also to move and displace their contents.

Let's go back to our categories and principles and see how they apply to pottery.

Lace Teapot

by Léopold L. Foulem

ceramic

1988

Credit: Huno

First principle: universality. All cultures make pottery. In the first category, crisis heterotopia, we had the motel room. A ceramic example could be the toilet bowl. (The bathroom itself is an interesting ceramic space. To use the language of contemporary criticism, it is site-specific as well as an installation, since all the diverse elements that compose that particular space are distinct yet in relation with each other.) In the second category, deviation heterotopia, we had retirement homes. A ceramic example could be the "vessel" in Paul Mathieu's *Garniture* (1990), this hybrid object where function has been transcended. I do not mean this in a derogatory way: I simply see vessels as the domain of the individual, the way prisons or psychiatric hospitals are for persons who do not fit with the norm (that is, tradition).

Second principle: change with context and culture. Thus a simple porcelain urinal can become one of modern art's most famous objects, and Marcel Duchamp's *Fountain* or a simple bowl can become a priceless work of art.

Third principle: juxtaposition. Pottery is probably the prime example of this principle. In a pot we find the exterior in complete symbiosis with the interior, the three-dimensional form with the two-dimensional surface, the cultural with the practical. Of all art forms, pottery is probably the only one where these seemingly contradictory aspects are so intimately (and literally) fused.

Fourth principle: relation to time. This principle also applies especially to pottery. The process of making pottery is totally dependent on time in a way significantly different from other processes and techniques. It is a diachronic activity taking place at different times, with drastic changes in between. Each step is transitory, and after the firing these changes are irreversible. The completed object becomes "eternal," for its nature as ceramics cannot be reversed.

Cooking is a somewhat similar process, but its results, contrary to those of pottery, can be, if not reversed, at least totally transformed. Clay is also totally transformed; after firing, there is no longer any clay but a new material with new properties. Of all art materials, is there another that transforms itself so completely? Of course, plastics. And they have also replaced clay in its long-privileged role. Pottery accumulates time and preserves it. For that reason we know of certain vanished cultures through their pots because they retain their identity through time. Our culture also has transitory pottery, the throw-away cup in paper or styrofoam. What will remain of our contemporary culture?

Fifth principle: accessibility and ritual. The relation between pottery and ritual is well known, and it is in this quality that makes pots "privileged, sacred places reserved for specific purposes," like the object that will probably best define our culture in future archeology, the toilet bowl, and that other ritual object, the coffee cup. But Foucault (1970, 48) writes that they "suppose a system of opening and closing that both isolates them, and makes them penetrable." Obviously pots have lids and spouts, but pots are also accessible because their vocabulary of forms – lip, body, foot, handle, and so on, refers to the human body. There is very little distance between a pot and a body since pots must be touched to be experienced. We all know that touching is art's ultimate taboo. But at the same time, pots are unpenetrable, difficult to understand. Their phenomenology is quite familiar and obvious, yet their epistemology is hardly accessible.

Foucault (1970, 48) expands on this notion of impenetrability in his book *The Order of Things* by comparing, on the one hand, utopias and representational, visual art with, on the other hand, heterotopias and representational pottery, whose purpose is not solely to represent life, but to participate in it. He writes:

> Utopias afford consolations: although they have no real locality, there is nevertheless a fantastic untroubled region in which they are able to unfold... Heterotopias are disturbing, probably because they secretly undermine language, because they make it impossible to name *this* or *that,* because they shatter and tangle common names, because they destroy syntax in advance, not only the one that constitutes sentences but the less apparent one that "holds together" (side by side and face to face) words and things.
>
> This is why utopias permit fables and discourses, they run with the very grain of language and are part of the very dimension of fabula; heterotopias... dessicate speech, stop words in their tracks, contest the very possibility of language at its source; they dissolve our myths and sterilize the lyricism of our sentences.

I believe that is the reason why pottery finds itself outside discourse, art criticism, and other institutional manifestations and why the ceramic aspects of Marcel Duchamp's *Fountain* are never considered: they are unmentionable. Of course, that is not the point of Duchamp's work. But it is my point. Why is it so seemingly easy to write about art and so difficult to do so about crafts? Most texts written about crafts are technical, historical, or subjectively philosophical. It is difficult to comprehend them otherwise. These objects are not easily deconstructed by theory and discourse. In our culture, since art is justified by theory and discourse, crafts can easily be ignored and rejected or, at least, their meaning misunderstood. This silence about craft functions like censorship to create a prohibition.

Recently we have also seen an amazing proliferation of images of pots in contemporary art, especially in painting and sculpture. Numerous examples come to mind, look at any art magazine. More than simple subject matter, these images (and an image can be three-dimensional), these representations of pottery do something extraordinary. They introduce heterotopias into the realm of utopias in a way similar to what happens, in reverse, when a landscape or figure is represented on a pot. Is the image of a pot on a pot a "homotopia" or a space representing itself?

The reason the art world has such difficulty in dealing with pottery (and other related practices) is not that pottery is not art. This opposition between art and craft is unnecessary and unproductive, although there is a real difference. The opposition stems from our habit of polarizing and opposing everything (black and white, good and bad, right and wrong, and so on). This smacks of morality and is quite useless. What is important to define is the grey zone where everything merges. In the field of art, craft is a heterotopia. It occupies a different space, another space, from the utopian practices of other art forms.

References

Foucault, Michel. 1986. "Of Other Spaces." *Diacritics* 16, no. 1 (Spring).
– – – 1970. *The Order of Things*. New York: Pantheon.
Mays, John Bentley. 1985. "Comment." *American Craft,* December-January 1985-86: 38-39.
Shadbolt, Doris. 1992. *Leadline Magazine* (published by Artists in Stained Glass, Toronto), 5.

Michel Paradis

Sémiotique de l'objet artisanal : Matière et sérialité comme lieux d'ancrage de la signification

Michel Paradis enseigne au

Département d'histoire de l'art, de l'Université

du Québec à Montréal.

The Semiotics of the Craft Object:
Matter and Seriality as Anchors for Signification

The problem of the signification of works of art from the standpoint of their production, while situating them in the practical reality of creation (that is, according to Étienne Souriau, looking at the concrete process that brings a thing into being with enough reality), has existed since the time of Aristotle. It was he who explicity launched the debate in his Metaphysics, when he tried to decide whether the individuation of the object produced by art was determined by matter or form. Though the question was not clearly answered by Aristotle or by any of the philosophers or practitioners who have followed to this day, the discussion surrounding it at least allows us to try to define the conditions that give craft production its distinctive character.

From a dyadic semiological perspective (sign-signifier/signified), the attempt to embody a reasonably well-defined form in a more or less resistant matter can be seen as the intention to produce signs. Adopting the hypothesis that an object thus produced is a sign, we can identify matter as the key semiotic shifter with respect to the production of crafts when we consider such production in relation to the question of a serial development in which redundance in matter is a determining criterion. A craftwork is, after all, usually defined in terms of the capacity of a given technique to "inform" a given matter with modulations that can be described in terms of tangible experience, and especially the capacity to repeat that process of informing by generating, more or less consciously, a number of variations. Thus, matter could represent the signifier in relation to the proposed signified but would also be the starting point of a system in which craft expression recovered the accident by which the attempt to repeat a model was transformed into the creation of new forms.

In the analysis of early Canadian artworks, such as wayside crosses and calvaries, weathercocks, and traditional pottery, the question of the distinctive character of craft production would find a new and useful theoretical basis in a proposed semiotics of craft techniques; that project is the main focus of my current research. This question also touches closely on the fundamental problem of the classification of craft and folk art in museums, as well as the characterization and reinterpretation of existing collections. This is one of the main criteria for the conservation and diffusion of this type of object.

On pourrait dire que notre cervelle contient non seulement les souvenirs acquis mais aussi, virtuellement, tous les souvenirs que nous pourrions avoir et que nous n'aurons jamais...

René Thom

1. Un calvaire anonyme...

En 1971, Jean Trudel procédait à l'analyse d'un Christ en croix de bois sculpté, oeuvre anonyme appartenant à la collection permanente du Musée des Beaux-Arts de Montréal. D'emblée, Trudel soulevait une question essentielle à laquelle il allait chercher à donner réponse dans les quelques lignes de son texte :

> On serait porté à lui coller l'étiquette «d'oeuvre primitive» sans plus chercher à définir pourquoi... Il serait cependant dangereux d'affirmer que le caractère primitif de l'oeuvre provient du manque de formation technique de celui que l'a exécutée.[1]

Poursuivant, l'auteur remarquait que cette oeuvre ne devait pas être considérée comme un «Christ mort suspendu à une croix et tirant de tout le poids

1 Trudel, Jean, «Une sculpture québécoise du dix-huitième siècle ramenée à Montréal», *Revue M*, vol. 2, no. 4, 1971, p. 5.

2 *Ibid.*

de son corps mort… flottant dans l'espace et dans le temps».[2] Puis, le comparant à une oeuvre similaire de Louis Jobin, un sculpteur québécois de formation,[3] il en tirait l'observation suivante:

> La sculpture de Jobin est une étude très fouillée faite d'après un modèle vivant et portant sur le corps d'un homme crucifié qui se trouve à être le Christ... La sculpture du Musée des Beaux-Arts est l'expression d'un concept du Christ en croix.[4]

Notre sculpteur, travaillant vraisemblablement, selon Trudel, d'après «une oeuvre antérieure qu'on lui avait donnée comme modèle»[5] serait donc arrivé, qu'il en ait été ou non conscient, à incarner dans une matière résistante (le bois), un concept, un être abstrait, reconnu par les chrétiens comme un signe de la Rédemption.

Pour ce sculpteur, le résultat sera sans doute allé bien au-delà de ses espérances. Trudel en effet, souligne comment la sculpture illustre puissamment «en la réduisant à l'essentiel» la vision d'un Christ en croix et «force l'attention du spectateur par son aspect sévère et dépouillé»[6] et John R. Porter parle de la «forte charge émotive dégagée».[7] Devant ces réactions, on serait porté à se demander quel est donc ce créateur qui a eu là si heureuse inspiration? quel est le contexte de production? comment celui-ci peut-il expliquer la genèse de l'oeuvre? etc. Bref, on souhaiterait en savoir davantage. Or en 1983, suite à une adroite recherche, la provenance de cette croix est établie, son auteur identifié : il s'agirait selon toute vraisemblance, d'une croix de calvaire sculptée au couteau, entre 1890 et 1910, par un cultivateur du nom de Pierre Plante pour son village de Sainte-Victoire, près de Sorel.[8] Fort de cette connaissance, on s'en doute, le Musée des Beaux Arts de Montréal révisa son attribution initiale de l'oeuvre à un artisan de la péninsule gaspésienne, attribution dont on nous dit qu'elle fut «sans doute motivée par l'aspect primitif de la représentation».[9]

Force nous est d'admettre qu'une fois réparée cette injustice de l'histoire de l'art, la connaissance du fait apparemment nouveau que représente cette

---

3 Le sculpteur Louis Jobin (1845-1928), élève de F. X. Berlinguet, lui-même fils de sculpteur et formé par Thomas Baillairgé, procède d'une «filières artistiques» les plus solidement établies du Québec ancien. Son art, s'apparentant à celui de François Baillairgé est décrit comme «académique et prolongeant jusqu'au XXe siècle le style en vogue dans la deuxième moitié du XIXᵉ siècle.»
Musée du Québec, *Le Musée du Québec, 500 oeuvres choisies,* Québec, (nov. 83 – mars 84), Gouvernement du Québec,1983, p. 119.

4 Trudel, loc. cit., p. 6.

5 *Ibid.*

6 *Ibid.*

7 Musée du Québec, *Le Grand Héritage, l'Eglise Catholique et les arts au Québec,* Québec (sept. 84 - janv. 85), Gouvernement du Québec, 1984, p. 284.

information, ne change finalement rien du tout à l'oeuvre elle-même. Il est toujours possible d'en souligner la puissance d'évocation mais aussi les mal-adresses anatomiques, et d'excuser son apparente gaucherie et son aspect primitif, par sa charge expressive. Rien de tout cela n'est modifié par la con-naissance documentaire que nous avons acquise en 1983, et qui ne fait que confirmer ce dont on se doutait déjà : l'auteur n'était pas un sculpteur de formation mais son oeuvre n'en demeure pas moins remarquable. En fin de compte, par ce processus, nous n'avons fait que démontrer que les méthodes traditionnelles de l'histoire de l'art (analyse formelle, stylistique, icono-graphique) sont efficaces dans les limites qui leur sont propres. Autrement dit, une méthode de description ne peut décrire que ce pourquoi elle a été conçue et rien de plus.

Pour reprendre le point de vue d'Albert Jacquard, en révélant du «nou-veau» qui n'était jamais que du préexistant, nous n'avons mis au jour aucun *supplément* à ce qui existait déjà.[10] Le nom du sculpteur, de même que le sou-venir de son oeuvre dans son contexte premier, existaient quelque part dans une «banque» de mémoires, et il y avait une certaine possibilité pour que ces données soient communiquées par ceux qui les détenaient à ceux qui cher-chaient à les obtenir, ce qui s'est finalement réalisé. Somme toute, le vérita-ble «nouveau» se situe bien d'avantage ici dans les effets que génère cette sculpture et qui la distinguent véritablement des centaines d'autres produites au Québec depuis deux ou trois siècles.[11] De là, découle la nécessité de regarder de plus près le processus concret qui amène l'objet à se manifester à nous, avec ce que le philosophe Etienne Souriau aurait décrit comme "un éclat suffisant de réalité"[12] et qui, en dernière analyse, caractérise ses *propriétés émergentes*[13] et engendre ce qu'on peut appeler des «effets de sens».

Revenons maintenant à la première remarque de Trudel, mise en exer-gue au début de ce texte : on est porté, en regardant le Christ en croix de Pierre Plante, à parler «d'oeuvre primitive» sans trop savoir pourquoi. Qu'en penser? Il me semble que la réponse se trouve précisément à la fin de l'analyse de Trudel, dans ces mots: « [l'auteur] transmettait une tradition sans

8 Lanthier, Monique, «Découverte de la provenance d'une croix de chemin», *Vie des arts*, vol. XXVII, no. 110, mars- avril- mai 1983, p. 60.

9 *Ibid*.

10 Jacquard, Albert, *L'héritage de la liberté*, Paris, Seuil, 1986, p. 78.

11 *Le Grand Héritage*, op. cit., p. 281 et note 26, p. 282.

12 Souriau, Etienne, *L'instauration philosophique*, Paris, Félix Alcan, 1939, p. 10.

13 Cette notion est définie comme l'apparition, dans la combinaison des éléments d'une structure donnée selon un ordre spécifique, de quelque chose de nouveau, absent de chacun des éléments pris séparément. Reeves, Hubert, *Malicorne,* Paris, Seuil, 1990, p. 111.

Calvaire

circa 1888, bois de pin et
polychrome, Pierre Plante (1853-1930).
Courtoisie de: Museé de beaux-arts,
Montréal, 1965.

le savoir et sa créativité se situait dans l'interprétation du modèle. Même sans connaître ce modèle, il est possible de dire que la part du sculpteur est très grande... ".[14] Bref, ce qui constitue un apport, une plus-value si l'on préfère, se situe précisément dans cette variation, cette *différentielle* entre une source présumée (mais non connue) et qu'on peut considérer comme une donnée initiale de l'artiste et le résultat final, la forme incarnée dans la matière que nous avons sous les yeux au Musée des Beaux-Arts de Montréal. En d'autres mots, cette différentielle qui se manifesterait à nous, notamment par une sorte de «primitivisme», c'est l'interprétation de l'auteur qui la produirait. Et cela, c'est précisément de la nouveauté, c'est-à-dire un ensemble d'effets qu'il eût été parfaitement impossible de prévoir sur la base des données initiales, fort nombreuses au demeurant, qui ont concouru à l'élaboration de notre calvaire.

Que l'on considère en effet les canons du Concile de Trente qui, au XVIe siécle fixèrent l'iconographie des images saintes en occident,[15] le modèle inconnu dont s'est peut-être servi l'artiste, l'esprit de compétition entre villages, qui a pu motiver l'érection de ce calvaire,[16] le matériau et la connaissance du travail de ce dernier qu'avait le sculpteur, son contexte et son patrimoine culturel, etc. L'on arrivera à la conclusion que la part d'imprévu pouvant surgir de l'ensemble de ces données était si grande qu'il y avait très peu de chances qu'il n'en émergeât pas du nouveau. Toutes les données initiales étaient parfaitement analysables individuellement, localement. Mais d'aucune nous n'aurions pu induire comme résultat global l'oeuvre de Plante. Ici, comme ailleurs, ont joué *nécessité et hasard*, un processus qu'Hubert Reeves décrit ainsi:

14 Trudel, loc. cit. p. 6.

15 Par exemple, en ce qui concerne les clous fixant le Christ sur la croix, Louis Réau signale que: «Dans les monuments du haut Moyen-âge, le corps du Christ est fixé par quatre clous, depuis le XIIIe siècle avec trois clous seulement, les deux pieds étant ramenés l'un sur l'autre. A partir de la Contre-Réforme on n'observe plus aucune règle... La doctrine du Concile de Trente laisse aux artiste toute latitude à cet égard.»
Réau, Louis, Iconographie de l'art chrétien, Paris, P.U.F., 1959, vol. II, p. 480.

16 Ainsi que le souligne Trudel «Il existait une forte rivalité entre les diverses paroisses du Québec en ce qui con cernait l'ornementation des églises».
Trudel, Jean, «Un aspect de la sculpture ancienne du Québec, le mimétisme», Vie des arts, été 1969, p. 33.
Nul doute qu'il en ait été de même pour les calvaires et croix de chemin, ainsi qu'on le note par exemple en Bretagne où les compétitions entre villages étaient parfois féroces lorsqu'il s'agissait d'ériger un monument religieux: «Il est arrivé à de riches paroisses voisines de Bretagne, qui se jalousaient et prétendaient vider entre elles la question de suprématie à coups de monuments religieux, de rivaliser sur ce plan, en calvaires à nom breux personnages».
Quefféfec, Henri, l'Evangile des calvaires bretons, Paris, Hachette, 1957, p. 12.

En résumé, pour comprendre un fait ou un événement, il faut connaître à la fois les lois physiques qui les régissent et les cadres dans lesquels ils se situent. Ces cadres impliquent le jeu d'autres lois dans d'autres cadres. De proche en proche, ces cadres et ces lois font intervenir tout l'univers, dans le temps et l'espace. C'est dans cette trame que s'insère le hasard.[17]

Pour utiliser une autre référence, issue cette fois des mathématiques fondamentales, je dirais que le Christ en croix de Pierre Plante constitue une *morphogénèse,* une *catastrophe* au sens où il s'agit de l'apparition de formes non prévisibles sur la base des données initiales, «l'expression par une discontinuité des propriétés du milieu».[18] Pourquoi se produit cette "catastrophe" que constitue le fait plastiquement nouveau par rapport à une iconographie déjà formée et quel est son sens dans le développement général des formes? Comment peut-on interpréter l'apparition d'une forme nouvelle en arts visuels et quels sont les enjeux de cette apparition? Telles sont les questions motivant cette présente réflexion. Je résumerai cette position par les mots de René Thom: «De l'examen macroscopique de le morphogénèse d'un processus, de l'étude locale ou globale de ses singularités, on s'efforcera de remonter à la dynamique qui l'engendre».[19]

Vers une sémiotique des qualités émergentes.

La question de la signification des objets d'art, en regardant le processus concret qui les amène à être en ce monde et surtout les effets spécifiques par lesquels cette arrivée à l'être marque le réel, n'est pas de celles que l'on peut écarter du revers de la main. Posé déjà par Aristote il y a plus de deux mille ans,[20] le problème consistant à déterminer ce qui, entre la matière et la

---

17 Reeves, Hubert, *Patience dans l'azur,* Québec, Québec Science Editeur, 1981, p. 197.
   Dans un autre texte, Reeves revient sur cette comparaison qu'on peut établir entre le processus créateur de la nature et celui de l'artiste: "Nous découvrirons… de surprenantes analogies entre l'activité de la nature et celle de l'artiste. Non seulement les deux jouent aux mêmes jeux, mais ils y jouent pratiquement dans les mêmes conditions."
   Reeves, *Malicorne,* op. cit., p. 143.

18 Thom, René, *Stabilité structurelle et morphogénèse,* Paris, Interéditions, 1977, pp. 9 et 324.

19 *Ibid.,* p. 8.

20 par exemple: "… ce qu'on appelle forme ou substance n'est pas engendré, mais ce qui est engendré, c'est le composé de matière et de forme, lequel reçoit son nom de la forme;… et tout être engendré renferme de la matière, une partie de la chose étant matière, et une autre partie, forme".
   Aristotle, *Métaphysique,* Z, 8, (1033 b).

forme, établit l'individuation de l'objet produit par l'art n'a bien sûr pas trouvé de solution ultime, à travers les nombreuses spéculations auxquelles il a donné lieu. Il peut cependant, tant est grande sa richesse, nous permettre d'envisager une réflexion sur la spécificité des productions dites artisanales et/ou populaires.

D'entrée de jeu, soyons clair : je ne chercherai pas ici à rejoindre la discussion qui, à travers les étiquettes d'art «naïf», «populaire», «traditionnel», «mineur» ou «majeur», s'efforce de caractériser la production de l'artiste et celle de l'artisan. Du point de vue des études en arts visuels, cette polémique fort ancienne me paraît être sans objet. Même si l'on admet que la connaissance des matières et techniques diffère entre «artistes savants» et «artisans», «qu'elle n'est pas soutenue par les mêmes institutions,... ne répond ni au même projet ni à la même position de l'homme dans le monde», il n'en demeure pas moins qu'il reste toujours un projet, une matière, une forme. Ainsi que le remarque fort pertinemment Louis Réau : «du point de vue iconographique, l'oeuvre d'un modeste artisan peut présenter autant ou même plus d'intérêt que la création d'un artiste de génie.»[22]

Je retiendrai cependant comme corpus de départ, toute production humaine d'objets esthétiques présentant un certain caractère de sérialité, c'est-à-dire des répétitions plus ou moins suivies de traits distinctifs dans un volume d'objets suffisamment important pour qu'on puisse l'observer qualitativement. J'ai conscience ici de la pauvreté de cette définition et de ses limites imprécises, mais, on s'en rappellera, mon problème consiste d'abord à étudier et comprendre des phénomènes de morphogénèse et comme point de départ, il me paraît utile de commencer mes investigations avec un nombre relativement limité de données initiales susceptibles de générer un très grand nombre de variations non prévues, quitte à resserrer ultérieurement les critères déterminants de ce corpus. Dans cet ordre d'idées, il me semble que ce qu'il est convenu d'appeler «l'artisanat» présente le caractère de sérialité recherché. C'est donc de ce côté que j'irai chercher mes premiers éléments d'étude, dans les calvaires et croix de chemin, par exemple, qu'on les désigne comme populaires, traditionnels ou autrement (mais cela pourrait être dans la poterie, la menuiserie, la broderie, etc.).

21 Cuisenier, Jean, *L'art populaire en France,* Paris, Arthaud, 1987, p. 76.

22 Réau, op. cit., T. 1, p. 3. Sur cette question, voir aussi :
    Paradis, Michel, "Modèles et sérialité: considérations sur quelques situations limites", section 1.1.2., (collectif des professeurs du département d'histoire de l'art de l'U.Q.A.M., à paraître prochainement.)

23 Focillon, Henri, *Le Moyen Age gothique,* Paris, Livre de Poche, 1971, p. 203.

Résumons. Nous avons maintenant une problématique et les fondements théoriques d'un corpus. On l'a dit, il n'est pas plus question de s'intéresser ici aux auteurs des oeuvres, en tant qu'individus particuliers, qu'aux sources qu'ont utilisé ces derniers au départ de leur élaboration. Peu nous importe donc qu'il s'agisse de Jacques, Jean ou Pierre Plante et que son modèle ait été une gravure, un tableau ou un autre calvaire. Seule nous intéresse ici l'apparition de qualités émergentes dans nos oeuvres et les effets de sens qu'elles produisent. Nous voici donc débarrassés du «despotisme de la référence»[23] et de «l'histoire de l'art par les influences». On évitera ainsi l'écueil d'avoir à excuser la maladresse d'une oeuvre dite artisanale par ses qualités expressives et tout le discours plus ou moins condescendant consistant à s'étonner de la réussite de telles oeuvres réalisées avec des moyens souvent rudimentaires.

Il faut maintenant adopter un principe méthodologique dans cette réflexion. Je le répète, il ne s'agit pas ici de redécouvrir ce qui est déjà bien connu, à savoir que les formes en arts visuels évoluent selon divers paramètres, mais bien de comprendre en quoi ces *informations nouvelles de la matière* sont significatives. De quoi sont-elles signe, et comment peut-on les interpréter précisément comme des porteuses de sens lorsqu'elles apparaissent? C'est précisément cette apparition du nouveau et ce qu'il signifie au moment où il se produit qui nous intéresse. Quels en sont les enjeux, comment le comprendre?

J'ai introduit le terme de *signe*, il y a quelques instants. Dès lors qu'on parle de signes, on parle de ce qui remplace autre chose, de ce qui est là précisément parce qu'autre chose n'y est pas. Mais qu'est-ce qui remplace? Qu'est-ce qui est remplacé? Pourquoi ce qui remplace est-il investi du pouvoir de substitution à ce qui est remplacé? Comment ce pouvoir de substitution s'exerce-t-il et quelle autorité en décide, etc. Tout cela forme le sens, et c'est bien de la *traque* de ce sens dont il est si difficile de parler, comme le souligne Algirdas J. Greimas,[24] qu'il s'agit dans cette réflexion. Chercher à débusquer ce qui, derrière les apparences, demeure caché et pourtant parlant, tel est ultimement l'objectif poursuivi.

24 Greimas, Algirdas J., *Du sens,* Paris, Seuil, 1970, p. 7.

Ainsi, une approche sémiotique pourrait-elle servir à interpréter ce qui se dissimule derrière l'apparition du nouveau dans les formes plastiques, en particulier dans celles qu'on dit artisanales, parce qu'elles ne sont pas régies par des règles strictes, par des normes édictées par l'autorité, mais demeurent fortuites et aléatoires, chaotiques et imprévisibles,[25] et parce qu'on ne sait pas vraiment pourquoi naissent ces nouvelles formes mais qu'il nous faut bien constater qu'elles émergent et se substituent aux anciennes. De quoi tiennent-elles lieu alors? C'est là me semble-t-il, que se situe le sens de ces oeuvres, dans ces écarts, cette différentielle dont j'ai déjà parlé et qu'on décrit habituellement comme «l'interprétation par rapport au modèle».[26]

Entre la forme et la matière, une dynamique du non prévu.

Eliminons donc ce modèle-source qui nous gêne si souvent dans nos interprétations parce que nous ne le retrouvons presque jamais et postulons que, dans une perspective sémiologique dyadique (signe, signifiant/signifié), le projet d'incarner dans une matière plus ou moins résistante, une forme plus ou moins déterminée, peut être ramené à une production de signes. Dans l'hypothèse selon laquelle l'objet produit et terminé serait un signe, on pourrait retenir, en ce qui concerne la pratique des métiers d'art, la matière comme embrayeur sémiotique privilégié, comme lieu d'ancrage de la sérialité. Le métier d'art ne se définit-il pas traditionnellement en fonction de la capacité d'un savoir-faire donné à «informer» une matière donnée de modulations caractérisables au niveau de l'expérience sensible et surtout, à la capacité de répéter cette information, en engendrant plus ou moins consciemment, un certain nombre de variations? La matière, dans cette approche, pourrait être vue comme un signifiant par rapport au projet-forme/signifié, mais aussi comme point de départ d'un système récupérant au bénéfice de l'interprétation personnelle de l'auteur, l'accident, la catastrophe transformant le projet initial en création de formes nouvelles, en morphogénèse. Dans cet esprit, nous pourrions aussi poser, suivant en cela

25 Vandevivere, Ignace, «Préface» à Foulon, Pierre-Jean, *La sculpture populaire: analyse d'un cas, le calvaire du bois du Grand Bon Dieu à Thuin,* Bruxelles, Ministère de la culture française, coll. Folklore et art populaire de Wallonie, vol. VII, 1972, p. vii.

26 «Tout le sens de son oeuvre [l'artiste populaire] tient aux écarts qu'elle présente par rapport au modèle. Bien loin de n'être que des défauts, ces différences ont souvent d'éminentes qualités expressives et reflètent les conditions particulières dans lesquelles l'oeuvre populaire a été créée.»
Foulon, Pierre-Jean, op. cit., p. 94.

27 Baudrillard, Jean, *Le système des objets,* Paris, Gallimard, 1984, p. 135.

Jean Baudrillard, que le modèle que nous avons éliminé tout à l'heure n'est pas à rechercher à l'extérieur du corpus mais à l'intérieur de ce dernier, dans la sommation des différences locales. Assumant le modèle comme «une image générique faite de l'assomption de toutes les différences relatives»[27], nous pourrions très bien concevoir chaque oeuvre comme sous-ensemble d'un modèle global théorique sans cesse en évolution et surtout comme le signe des relations qui s'établissent entre le projet de création (qui n'est au fond pas autre chose que d'ajouter au modèle global en évolution) et la matière impliquée dans cette création. La forme se développerait au prix d'une auto-amplification de ces relations, dont le résultat final demeurerait dès lors totalement imprévisible.[28]

Prenons un exemple concret. John R. Porter donne, pour le Québec ancien, quatre critères en vertu desquels l'auteur d'une oeuvre sur bois sélectionnait son matériau :

> Loin d'être le fruit du hasard, le choix du créateur était fonction de quatre grands facteurs, soit le lieu d'exécution de la pièce, son lieu d'exposition, son utilisation et son traitement de surface.

Ces critères, qu'on considérera comme des données initiales, pèseront lourdement sur le développement des formes en se renforçant mutuellement et, au gré des circonstances, en venant interagir plus ou moins activement avec d'autres données. Ainsi, Porter remarque que :

> Dans le cas d'une oeuvre exposée à l'intérieur, le sculpteur pouvait délibérément utiliser un bois noueux, s'il était prévu qu'une dorure ou une polychromie de qualité viendrait cacher les imperfections de surface.[30]

Comme on le voit, une des conditions initiales, le traitement de surface, amène le choix d'un bois nécessitant une certaine technique de travail, ce qui est susceptible de modifier le projet-forme initial. Une relation projet-matière non prévue, une discontinuité, risque de se manifester. Ainsi, de l'usage d'un savoir-faire particulier utilisé pour affronter une matière choisie

---

28 Cela supposerait l'existence d'une «boucle de rétroaction»: «La cause produit l'effet, et l'effet modifie la cause, modifiant ainsi l'effet, etc.»

Reeves, Hubert, op. cit., p. 100.

Sur cette base, et au bout d'un temps assez court, plus rien n'est prévisible. On parle alors d'horizon prédictif très court. Il faut cependant bien se rappeler que ceci n'est effectif *qu'à condition que la cause soit sensible à l'effet* .

29 Porter, John R. et Bélisle, Jean, *La sculpture ancienne au Québec,* Montréal, Editions de l'Homme, 1986, p. 23.

30 *Ibid.*

en fonction d'une contrainte spécifique du projet, apparaîtront des imperfections qui, à leur tour, pourront générer de nouvelles formes. Du connu, analysable en ses composantes particulières, surgira l'imprévu, naîtra un nouveau «système de matière».[31]

Si l'on considère les impacts profonds que peuvent avoir les données initiales sur la création de formes nouvelles, on est fondé à postuler que d'une façon générale, les liens qui s'établissent entre le projet et la matière, ne peuvent que conduire à «un mouvement incessant de naissance, de développement, de destructions de formes»[32] et c'est ce mouvement qui, me semble-t-il, découpé en ses instances particulières, s'avérera finalement porteur de sens.

Ces conditions initiales dont j'ai parlé, les historiens d'art les ont depuis longtemps repérées et signalées. Mais ils ne les ont que peu utilisées, autrement que comme critères typologiques, par exemple dans des perspectives économiques, esthétiques, historiques, sociologiques, stylistiques, etc. C'est avec ce type de descripteurs que sont habituellement classées les collections muséales. Il me semble qu'il faut maintenant les approcher en tant qu'embrayeurs de sens, en leur permettant de révéler comment, dans le perpétuel jeu qui se noue entre le créateur et la matière, se construisent, s'incarnent et se substituent les uns aux autres, des effets de sens qui «... se conformant à la nature de la réalisation, conquièrent peu à peu le don de la réalité».[33] C'est là, je pense, que les arts visuels prennent sens. Du moins, est-ce là qu'on peut espérer le découvrir.

Dans l'objectif de réinterpréter des corpus en art canadien ancien tels les calvaires et croix de chemin, les coqs de clocher ou les poteries traditionnelles, la question de la spécificité de l'artisanat trouverait donc un ancrage théorique intéressant et nouveau dans le projet d'une sémiotique des pratiques en métiers d'arts. En ouvrant de nouvelles avenues d'interprétation des artefacts en leurs effets caractéristiques, cette question touche aussi le problème de la classification des objets artisanaux et d'art populaire en milieu muséal ainsi que la caractérisation et la relecture des collections déjà constituées, qui demeure un des critères majeurs de la conservation et de la diffusion de ce type d'objets.

31 Cuisenier, op. cit., p. 80.

32 Thom, op. cit., p. 1.

33 Souriau, op. cit., p. 19.

Enfin, dans un ordre d'idées un peu différent, la perspective proposée pourrait permettre une nouvelle approche de corpus présentant des similitudes de développement avec les arts populaires et l'artisanat. Je pense en particulier aux arts plastiques des périodes dites «de décadence» où l'irruption non prévue de nouveaux éléments visuels est assez fréquente, par exemple, comme l'a souligné André Grabar, dans les débuts de la période paléochrétienne.[34]

34 Grabar a souligné ce problème en mettant en lumière les raisons habituellement données à ces modifications de formes : les maladresses d'artisans provenant d'ateliers excentriques et s'efforçant de s'adapter aux modèles dominants de l'esthétique classique encore toute proche dans le temps ; l'incompréhension des sources anciennes par certains créateurs «décadents» ; les influences d'autres cultures tendant à s'épanouir en raison de la dégradation de la culture initiale, etc. Refusant de suivre ces avenues, l'auteur préfère mettre en évidence un double phénomène d'intégration graduelle de formes nouvelles dans l'esthétique d'un espace-temps donné puis de substitution consciente de cette nouvelle esthétique à l'ancienne : «Nous ne prenons pas position ici, dans ce débat sur l'origine du refus partiel de maintenir le canon classique, parce que seule nous intéresse actuellement la façon dont le style nouveau a servi aux artistes pour interpréter des thèmes que l'art antique avait ignorés.» Ainsi peut-il, sans chercher à l'expliquer davantage, étayer une dynamique reconnue par des observations qui permettent d'aller plus loin dans la description d'une dynamique nouvelle.

Grabar, André, «Le message de l'art byzantin», dans *Les origines de l'esthétique médiévale,* Paris, Macula, 1992, p. 20 et «Le tiers monde de l'Antiquité à l'école classique et son rôle dans la formation de l'art du Moyen Age», dans *L'art paléochrétien et l'art byzantin,* Londres, Variorum Reprints, 1979, pp. 1- 59.

Michele Hardy

Crafts and Knowledge

Michele Hardy is a graduate
student in Clothing and Textiles at the
University of Alberta in Edmonton.

Artisanat et savoir

Cet article traite du recoupement des divers moyens d'accéder à la connaissance et du défi que représente un savoir fondé sur l'expérience de l'artisanat dans le cadre d'une vision rationaliste du monde. Les féministes et les personnes autochtones ont illustré l'exclusion et la fausse représentation dont elles ont toutes deux été victimes et qui découlent de cette vision du monde dominante (Code 1991; Harding 1987; Rose 1984). Ces thèmes suggèrent qu'il existe de multiples façons d'être et de connaître basées sur des expériences variées du monde (Code 1991; Ridington 1982, 1988). Dans cet exposé, j'aborde les similitudes qui unissent le féminisme, le savoir indigène et l'artisanat, et je soutiens que l'artisanat constitue une perspective particulière. Je défends la thèse d'un savoir artisanal issu d'une relation spécifique et intime entre l'artisan, les matériaux, les techniques, l'esthétique et le but recherché. Je crois que l'artisanat suppose une compréhension particulière du monde.

Tout comme le féminisme et le savoir indigène, l'artisanat privilégie l'expérience et le rôle joué par le «sujet» qui vit l'expérience. Ce que l'on connaît à titre d'artisan ne peut être dissocié de la manière par laquelle on le connaît. Le savoir artisanal part d'une expérience réelle et vécue. Comme artisans, notre connaissance est cérébrale et tactile, elle provient à la fois de l'intellect et du corps tout entier. La connaissance artisanale est

I would like to thank Dr. Sandra Niessen for her advice and encouragement in the preparation of this paper.

vécue, intuitive, esthétique et intellectuelle. Elle revêt une compréhension du monde distincte qui s'appuie sur cette expérience. Ceci conteste l'autorité du savoir rendu par des observateurs objectifs de la méthode scientifique et, par le fait même, remet en question le positivisme exclusif de la pensée intellectuelle occidentale.

L'Académie a à peine reconnu, et encore moins accepté, la validité «d'autres» manières de connaître le monde. Les métiers d'art ont ainsi fait l'objet de marginalisation et de fausse représentation. L'Académie ne parle pas le même langage et elle ne privilégie pas les mêmes résultats. L'artisanat est perçu comme une denrée tandis que les artisans sont représentés comme de «simples» techniciens. Cette concentration sur l'aspect tangible fait abstraction de la plénitude et de la spécificité de la connaissance artisanale. L'artisanat est de plus lié à un passé préindustriel révolu. Dans cette communication, je fais part de la nature de la connaissance artisanale et du défi qu'elle pose, non seulement à l'Académie, mais à notre propre vision de nous-mêmes. Par l'apprivoisement d'un dialogue et l'étude de ce que nous savons à titre d'artisans, je crois que nous pouvons proposer de nouvelles manières d'être, faire progresser la validité et le statut de l'artisanat et l'ancrer fermement dans le présent vivant sans négliger son potentiel pour l'avenir.

When I sit down to my sewing machine and prepare to work, everything must be right before I can proceed. Of course my materials must be at hand and my tools available and in working order. A pot of tea is usually handy. There are subjective factors involved as well. My ideas must be ripe or, rather, animated – they may yet be unformed but ready to focus and create. I cannot begin a new project until my ideas, materials, and tools fit together – not like a jigsaw puzzle, flat or static, but as something generative and unbounded.

There are many parallels between this way of working and the intent of this paper. It is a meditation on the real value of craft – value in a contemporary and holistic sense. This is new ground that I can only begin to glimpse, but the materials are assembled, connections tentatively formed, and my perspective as a craftsperson conscious and clear. At the heart of this paper is the premise that the nature of one's engagement with the world shapes one's perspective, or rather, *what* we know is contingent on *how* we know. The first step to reaching this new ground is to recognize the specificity of our engagement as craftspeople. A story within a story within a story – this paper explores the continuing development of my awareness of craft as a way of knowing the world, as a body of knowledge, and the implications of this.

This story begins, then, not with my training in textile crafts or my experience as craftsperson and instructor, but with my return to university. Plunged into an environment which privileges received knowledge, I craved the direct experiences I was used to. I longed to touch the artifacts I was studying, not with gloves, but directly with my skin. I pondered and probed those artifacts, not so much as illustrations, but as facts in themselves. I sensed in them not just representations of distant cultures, but something of the logic of their materials and manufacture.

Since I entered graduate school, my knowledge of textiles has repeatedly been challenged. Because it has developed through intensive and extensive experience with cloth, there are few course numbers and no marks to qualify it as tangible. Stultified by a mindset I could not yet name, I similarly could not question its validity or authority. It was not until I became familiar with feminist theory and with feminist critiques of science and philosophy that I began to recognize my experience and name my frustrations. These are that, as a woman and a craftsperson, I have felt insignificant, devalued, and guilty of self-indulgence both generally and specifically within the university. My experience with textiles was excluded and discounted as knowledge by a system for which science and objectivity are pre-eminent in the discovery of knowledge. My frustration was latent and unnamed because I could not see credible alternatives to this established value system. Feminism has thus helped me to recognize the value of my experience with textiles and, furthermore, to realize that alternatives are possible.

Experience has played a crucial role in the development of feminist thought. The first wave of feminism introduced women as worthy objects of study, encouraging reflection on the nature of women's experience and the source of the oppression they experience. With the recognition that women's voices were seldom heard and their interests not always protected, feminists began to challenge the hegemony of the dominant discourses (Harding 1990). The second wave of feminism began to expose the insidious implications of patriarchy and to question whether these established modes of thought could accommodate women. Feminists' recent critiques of philosophy and science have encouraged a re-evaluation of experience per se and its relationship with the construction of knowledge (Hawkesworth 1989; Haraway 1988; Code 1991). Together with post-modernism, feminist critiques have turned to deconstructions aimed at dismantling the mechanisms of exclusion and have insisted on women as the *subjective possessors* of knowledge (Harding 1987; Gross 1986; Code 1991).

Feminists have thus critiqued both the form and the content of science and philosophy. Objectivity, "pure" reason, and empiricism are the means of understanding privileged by the scientific method. Vision is the primary tool of the scientist in his search for truth. Supposedly unclouded by emotion or bias, this vision is uni-directional and non-interactive, and it assumes a passive, objective, and therefore observable reality. Severing the subject from the object, science heightens the distance between man and nature, contributing to a dichotomous conception of reality. Objectivity is pitted against subjectivity, intellect against feeling. The scientist is thus autonomous but alienated, privileging theory over experience, the quantitative over the qualitative, detachment over responsibility.

Feminists have disputed the assumptions upon which scientific knowledge rests. They question the possibility of objectivity and point out that the exclusion of women from the ranks of science betrays a subjectivity it will not admit. In her book *What Can She Know?* the feminist philosopher Loraine Code discusses the exclusion of women and their "traditional" skills from who counts as knowers and what counts as the known:

> The withholding of authoritative epistemic status from the knowledge *women* have traditionally constructed out of their designated areas of experience affords a peculiarly salient illustration of gender politics at work. "Gossip," "old wives tales," "women's lore," "witchcraft" are just some of the labels patriarchal societies attach to women's accumulated knowledge and *wisdom*... Its subjugation and trivialization can be explained only in terms of the structures of power and differential authority encoded in the *purity* demanded by ideal objectivity. This knowledge cannot attain that standard, the supposition is, because it grows out of experiences, out of continued contact with particularities of material, sensory objects – and it is strongly shaped by the subjectivity of its knowers: women. (Code 1991, 68, 69)

With the recognition of, first a woman's perspective, then women's perspectives, the authority of science to name universal truths has been eroded. The early feminists sought to determine the essence of a women's point of view, an idea gradually replaced with the recognition of multiple views. "Woman," for example, has been shown to be a category constructed within a particular context. Women of colour and women of the third world and the fourth are claiming their right to determine their identities, their agendas, and their feminisms (Mohanty 1988; Amos and Parmer 1984). (Fourth world refers to indigenous and minority women of the Western industrialized countries.) The struggles of native peoples for self-determination in this country poignantly illustrate the clash of two very different ways of knowing and therefore of "proving" land ownership: contractual agreements as opposed to the demonstration of extensive and intimate knowledge of land use. These examples suggest that there are many ways of knowing and many points of view and that there are many knowers unrecognized and devalued by science and the philosophies modelled on science. Value, including moral value, has been restricted to a very narrow and problematic way of knowing.

The pitting of subject against object forces a dualist conception of the world, one in which only half of the pair is credible. Black or white, sink or swim – these are the poles of late capitalist society. Female/male, nature/culture, subjective/objective – these are the axes upon which intellectual thought has turned. The feminism I embrace and believe should influence any consideration of craft is not one intent on sacrificing a patriarchal scapegoat or creating a cult of essential victimhood. Rather it is a feminism that acknowledges and explores the potent grey areas between the poles. It is a feminism which is critically aware of the hierarchies and biases resulting from science's monopoly on knowledge. It is one which fosters a "discursive space" (Gross 1986, 204) for exploring multiple possibilities and for re-evaluating the importance of personal experience and the subjective in the construction of knowledge. Code (1991, 47) suggests, for example, that both "emotion and intellect are mutually constitutive and sustaining, rather than oppositional forces in the construction of knowledge." She concludes her discussion of the possibility of a feminist epistemology by opting for a well-mapped middle-ground, one that "offers a place to take up positions of strength and maximum productivity from which exclusionary theories can be tapped critically and creatively for criticism and reconstruction" (p. 318).

This middle ground between the dichotomies that have dominated Western thinking offers a place to share ideas and tap new potential. Craft, though traditionally relegated to the hinterland rather than to a middle ground, can legitimately take a place in this creative milieu.

Earlier I expressed some of the frustration I have felt as a craftsperson and a woman. Through feminism I have begun to recognize the specificity and value of my perspective and understand the mechanisms which prevented me from doing so. This has been enormously empowering. Through this paper I am hoping to shed some light on the situation of craft. Mirroring my own experiences, craft is a marginalized, trivialized enterprise, more

Victorian Vessels, 1990
by Michele Hardy
silk, cotton, synthetic materials,
thread, wire, paint

**Unknown Woman with
Rarified Vessels,** 1990
by Michele Hardy
polyester and nylon materials,
thread, wire, paint

**Detail of
Rarified Vessels,** 1990
by Michele Hardy
polyester and nylon materials,
thread, wire, paint

often connected with an extinct pre-industrial past than the present. Craftspeople are like relics from another age – part technicians, part magicians. Crafts are discussed according to their tangible techniques, their products, or the subjective experience of the craftsperson. The "maker's hand" supposedly manipulates materials in a prescribed way according to the nature of the medium. The difference between art and craft has traditionally been the cognitive transcendence of the material and function of art. Craft remains tied to necessity and to the maker's hand, as opposed to the maker's intellect. The artist is credible because he transcends the particularities of materiality and discovers truth within himself. The craftsperson cannot claim the same transcendence and is therefore denied the same status. Feminism has demonstrated, however, that the means of assigning epistemic, moral, and economic value have been predicated by an objective, scientific model; therefore we should reject this characterization of the unknowing craftsperson. Feminism has furthermore opened up the potential to consider multiple possibilities and a range of ways of knowing. Code (1991) has suggested, for example, intuitive, experiential, and aesthetic ways of knowing.

From my experience as a craftsperson, I am claiming that craft is a particular engagement with the world, a particular way of knowing the world, and that it has a particular, though possibly non-verbal, known. I am also claiming that there are many benefits to exploring crafts as knowledge and as a way of knowing – benefits that are not easily quantifiable but that do have implications for life on this planet.

Let me draw on some of my experience for you. As a child I could not wait to sew. The attraction was not so much being able to use a sewing machine as it was the creative possibilities and the autonomy it presented. It was not until sometime later, after I had become competent and comfortable technically, that the textiles themselves grabbed me and I became intensely aware of their tactile qualities. Later the relationship of physical structure and drape sparked my imagination. Most recently colour, light, transparency, and opacity have intrigued me. Each new discovery overwhelms me with possibilities – it is like seeing cloth anew each time. My technical skills pace, and keep pace with, this evolving awareness of cloth. They are a means of manipulating and thinking with textiles.

My knowledge of cloth is of both the head and the fingertips of the intellect and the whole body. It is derived not only from academic study, but also from intensive and extensive experience. I can identify different fibres by touch. I can tell how a certain fabric will drape or wear – how it will look made up. I can imagine vividly how a fabric will feel on my body, whether it is a cool breezy wisp of silk pongee or the crisp dryness of cotton percale. I can describe how my scissors slice finely into silk or clump their way through a bulky woolen tweed. I can also describe the squeal of moiré or taffeta as I run a fingernail over it and the dull wave-like rumble and crash of a heavy rug being shaken. Similarly, I could describe the faint, sweet, acrid smell of indigo or the briny earthiness of new wool. There is a certain empathy among the senses – I can feel a fabric, know how it will drape and sound, *visually*. Furthermore, I can remember colours and textures and create with them in my mind.

The particularity of my experience with textiles predicates a particular engagement with the world. The known of craft, the skills and qualities it engenders, shapes our awareness and interactions. A craft knowledge includes the whole body sensitivity I have described above. It is not just an awareness like some super-sensitive sixth sense and is certainly more than just technique. If we have been unable to articulate this knowledge, it is as much a limitation of language (Miller 1987) as it is the failure of established epistemology to recognize both subjectivity and objectivity as components of the construction of knowledge.

The mindset which privileges scientific objectivism similarly privileges the mastery of the media that art engenders – the medium is harnessed, manipulated, or perfected by the artist's vision. Craft encourages sensitivity and empathy for one's medium. This burl of wood, lump of clay, or skein of yarn is not simply the "object" upon which skills are worked. They are *mediums* and thus active in the sense that they determine, develop, and change throughout a process, requiring minute, subtle reactions and decisions by the craftsperson. The division of subject and object engendered by science and art is not the case between craftsperson and medium. Craftsperson, medium, tools – they are of one unified gesture of creativity – their boundedness is less metaphysical than physical. Ursula Franklin (1990, 95) reminds us that when we uncritically accept objective rationalism, "the logic of technology begins to overpower and displace other types of social logic, such as the logic of compassion or the logic of obligation, the logic of ecological survival or the logic of linkages into nature."

Whereas a scientific vision views the world passively and disinterestedly, a craft way of seeing admits its subjectivity and is comprehensive in its awareness. Code (1991, 145) notes, "Brought to bear on observations of the natural world, this kind of seeing could signal a more respectful relation with nature, [and] a greater care for its peculiarities, than objective observation admits." A craft perspective is therefore potentially more responsible to the medium and its source because of the nature of its engagement.

Craft engenders another responsibility – the responsibility of the object. I recently read an account of Navaho aesthetics which moved me very deeply. Beauty to the Navaho is tied to the effectiveness or benefit of the object – a conceptual experience as opposed to a strictly perceptual one (Anderson 1990, 106). This goes beyond the idea of beauty received by the eye of the beholder to a more holistic experience uniting the mind, the eye, and the body. If beauty has been trivialized by Western society it is because it is restricted to physical beauty. The beauty of craft is not restricted to its isolated formal characteristics but includes consideration of production, materials, time, and place. I argue that craft is beautiful furthermore because it is beneficial – not just for the individual craftsperson, but through the creation of objects which engender a responsible relationship with nature and which celebrates the potential of a human maker.

In this paper I have tried to illustrate with my own experience the lessons we as craftspeople can learn from feminist critiques of science and philosophy. Feminism has opened the door to the consideration of many possibilities for knowing the world – craft represents a particular perspective. Questioning the values and aims implicit to science, feminism has furthermore demonstrated that these other points of view have value. The value of craft involves technical expertise, sensitivity, creativity, and a comprehensive awareness which acknowledges responsibility for process, materials, and product. A craft perspective is one with benefit, one therefore with beauty, and one whose specificity needs to be discussed. By recognizing the particulars of this perspective, the value of our knowledge, and its challenge to objectivity, in other words by becoming empowered to see and understand who we are as craftspeople, we can begin to break the shackles of romanticism and nostalgia and begin to weave, carve, forge, or throw a vital, more central and current role for craft. A recognition of our perspectives and the credibility of our knowledge is a first step toward this more wholesome middle ground.

References

Amos, V. and Parmer, P. 1984. "Challenging Imperial Feminism." *Feminist Review* 17: 3-19.

Anderson, R.L. 1990. *Calliope's Sisters: A Comparative Study of the Philosophies of Art.* Englewood Cliffs: Prentice Hall.

Code, L. 1991. *What Can She Know?* Ithaca: Cornell University Press.

Franklin, U.M. 1990, August 28. "Let's Put Science under a Microscope. *The Globe and Mail.*

Gross, E. 1986. "Conclusion: What is Feminist Theory?" In C. Pateman and E. Gross, eds., *Feminist Challenges: Social and Political Theory,* 190 203. Boston: Allen and Unwin.

Haraway, D. 1988. "Situated Knowledges: The Science Question in Feminism and the Privilege of Partial Perspective." *Feminist Studies* 14, 575-599.

Harding, S. 1987. "Introduction: Is There a Feminist Method?" In S. Harding, ed., *Feminism and Methodology,* 1-14. Bloomington: Indiana University Press.

– – – 1990. "Feminism, Science, and the Anti-enlightenment Critiques." In L.J. Nicholson, ed., *Feminism/Postmodernism,* 83-106. New York: Routledge.

Hawkesworth, M.E. 1989. "Knowers Knowing Known: Feminist Theory and Claims of Truth." *Signs* 14, 533-557.

Miller, D. 1987. *Material Culture and Mass Consumption.* Oxford: Blackwell.

Mohanty, C. 1988. "Under Western Eyes: Feminist Scholarship and Colonial Discourses." *Feminist Review* 30, 61-88.

Kathy M'Closkey – Respondent

Towards a Language of Craft

Kathy M'Closkey is a doctoral candidate

in the Department of Social Anthropology at York

University in Toronto. The title of her dissertation

is "Myths, Markets and Metaphors: Navajo Weaving

as a Commodity and Communication Form."

Résumé

Les catégories «art» et «métiers d'art» n'ont pris leur acception actuelle qu'à partir de la Renaissance. Depuis, l'histoire des métiers d'art est définie par son exclusion de l'histoire de l'art. Mon exposé s'attache à montrer comment est apparue cette distinction, à l'aide de renseignements tirés de l'esthétique et de l'histoire de l'art classiques, critiques et féministes. La compréhension critique de ce phénomène détruit à la base la justification des pratiques hégémoniques qui ont cours dans les grandes institutions culturelles actuelles.

Le céramiste québécois Paul Mathieu s'attaque à l'énigme que constitue le fait qu'on exalte l'art et les métiers d'art traditionnels aux dépens des métiers d'art contemporains. Il nourrit son essai de son expérience personnelle et reproche au monde des arts d'escamoter avec légèreté les métiers d'art. Paul Mathieu choisit de situer les métiers d'art parmi les hétérotopies complexes et embrouillées du monde réel, ainsi que le propose Michel Foucault. Mais Foucault oppose le monde «réel» au monde «idéal», utopique, de l'art visuel figuratif. Il me semble qu'en acceptant l'opposition que fait Foucault entre le «réel» (le physique) et l'»idéal» (le conceptuel), il cède à cette dichotomie qui a, en premier lieu, contribué à dévaluer les métiers d'art.

Michele Hardy, artiste qui travaille les textiles, se situe dans une perspective fémin-
iste ancrée dans la praxis, dans la pratique. Dans le passé, en insistant sur la nature concrète de l'objet artisanal, on a refusé de voir la primauté de la connaissance tacite
qu'implique sa production, connaissance indispensable à la création de toute forme
d'expression, quel qu'en soit le moyen.

Michel Paradis, Québécois spécialiste de l'histoire de l'art, fait appel à la sémiologie
pour élaborer un «langage» des métiers d'art, à propos d'une croix de l'artiste populaire
Pierre Plante. Il reprend la notion aristotélicienne d'hylémorphisme, union de la matière
et de la forme. Paradis propose de considérer la matière comme signifiant et la forme
comme signifié. Reprenant des notions élaborées dans la théorie de la communication,
je propose de considérer les métiers d'art, en tant que manifestations tangibles de relations humaines, comme des formes non verbales de la communication. C'est pourquoi
les analyses basées sur la linguistique (couple signifiant-signifié) ne peuvent pertinemment s'appliquer à des formes non verbales de communication.

As discussant I will respond first to questions raised in Paul Mathieu's essay
and describe briefly the genesis of the distinction between art and craft,
which reflects attitudes deeply rooted in Western philosophy and epistemology. A critical understanding and elaboration of how this distinction
emerged subverts the continued justification of hegemonic practices in
major cultural institutions today. Secondly I will discuss the importance of
tacit knowledge, beautifully addressed by Michele Hardy, and then finish with
a critique of semiotics as applied to craft, the subject of Michel Paradis's essay.

In his provocative text *Europe and the People without History*, the anthropologist Eric Wolf (1982, 388) remarks, "The ability to bestow meaning –
to 'name' things, acts and ideas – is a source of power. Control of communication allows the managers of ideology to lay down the categories through
which reality is to be perceived." The categories "art" and "craft" are not a
"god-given division," but are cultural constructions. They did not take on
their present meanings until the Renaissance. In the following section, I
summarize two years of study in classical, critical, and feminist art history
and aesthetics. This research composed the theoretical portion of my master's thesis in sociology, in which I returned to university to try to discover
how this insidious distinction began.[1]

During the Middle Ages, distinctions were noted among persons working in artisanal guilds, but there was no difference of prestige between arts

1 This distinction was the primary justification for merchant traders to market all Navajo weaving by
weight for eighty years (1880-1960). Well over half a million blankets and rugs were sold in this manner. Categories *do* make a differences.

and crafts. However, European tradition specified painters as primary designers because they alone had the ability to *designare* – draw, compose, and create. During the Renaissance, painters and sculptors spent years perfecting their ability to imitate nature and to reproduce the classical ideal in statuary and paintings inspired by the Greeks and Romans (Hauser 1965; Kristeller 1951; Pevsner 1940). During the Renaissance, "designare" increasingly emphasized a thorough knowledge of architecture, geometry, perspective, arithmetic, and anatomy (Pevsner 1940, 84).

The institutional separation of art from craft developed when painters and sculptors severed their association with the guilds in the mid-sixteenth century and joined the newly formed art academies headed by members of the nobility (Kristeller 1952, 54). This division reflects the duality of mental and manual labour enshrined in Western thought. The Greeks initiated this division by emphasizing mathematics as the first purely intellectual activity (the more mathematics involved in a job, the less manual it is) (Sohn-Rethel 1977, 103). But they never extended it to the realm of art. Painting and sculpture involved manual labour only. The Greeks esteemed poetry and music, and their term for "art" and its Latin equivalent were applied to all kinds of human activity. Painting and sculpture were two of the imitative arts (Kristeller 1951, 504). The privileging of mathematics (most early Greek philosophers were also mathematicians) created an unbridgeable dividing line between mental and manual labour in the West.

The application of mathematical principles to painting dramatically affected the status of the painter. Since they were able to construct an organized spatial system based on mathematics, painters became the doyens of the Enlightenment. This phenomenon is reflected in Leonardo da Vinci's treatise disseminated in the sixteenth century in which he likened painting to science and described the painter as god-like since he could depict on canvas that which God had created on earth (Clark 1967, 74-75). Drawing became the hallmark of "artistic literacy," but it also provided the means to dictate to others what would be produced. The concept of the artist as a unique, outstanding individual developed in contrast to the view that the anonymous craftsperson, using only technical ability, executed designs specified by someone else. Hence fine art became primarily an intellectual exercise, whereas the essence of craft production resided in the technical excellence of the completed piece. This demarcation between art and craft coincides with the birth of modern capitalism and the emergence of art as a commodity and speculative asset (Hauser 1965).

The principle common to all arts was the "imitation of beautiful nature," that is, realism. Abbé Bateaux codified the modern system of the fine arts in a treatise published in 1746. He divided the five fine arts of painting, sculpture, architecture (the visual arts) and poetry and music (including dance) from the mechanical arts (Kristeller 1952, 20). The discipline of aesthetics which emerged during this period canonized the distinction between art and craft by focusing on beauty as expressed only in non-utilitarian objects. The discipline itself consisted of the study of beauty and of the standards by which it was judged. Originally aesthetics referred to a theory of sensory perception; ultimately it referred only to sight. Classical aesthetics claimed that vision was superior to other senses because of its detachment from its objects. Kant's notion of the sublime applied only to painting and sculpture, as non-utilitarian objects, excluding of course, nearly everything created by human beings working in other media.

By the beginning of the nineteenth century, a number of influential German writers and philosophers, including Goethe, Hegel, and Kant, had published major treatises on aesthetics (Kristeller 1952). Kant himself reinforced the notion of the division of mental and manual labour by presenting it as a transcendental necessity. In his famous treatise *The Critique of Judgement,* Kant postulated an absolute opposition between labour and art. He saw labour as a forced, unpleasant activity. Art, however, was "production through freedom" (Kant 1951, 146). Only "play" (art) could act as mediator to reconcile the formal dichotomy between mind and body, reason and emotion. Otherwise these impulses were irreconcilable (Sohn-Rethel 1977). Kant's dictum "the necessary (or functional) cannot be judged beautiful, but only right or consistent" was the kiss of death for crafts and determined the path for an aesthetic that continues to predominate in many circles today. The philosophical tradition perpetuated by Kant and his contemporaries is itself a production of this division that originated in Greek philosophy – a preserve of intellectuals for intellectuals. The reconciliation of the dichotomy (through art) is an intellectual process.

All crafts suffered a double punishment, for not only were they equated with manual and functional activities and needs, compared to art, which symbolized the intellectual and non-utilitarian, but the status of craftspeople was further diminished when a major portion of all manual activity was replaced by machines (Thompson 1980). The creation of art since the Renaissance has occupied the attention of art critics, historians, aestheticians, academies and artists themselves. The history of craft has been shaped by its exclusion from art history. We know that craft objects do not vanish of their own volition – their disappearance is socially created and constantly reaffirmed by the gatekeepers of classical art history and aesthetics. Yet even today the titles of exhibitions which feature crafts still reinforce the predominant idea that only manual labour is needed: "From Our Hands," "Hands and Hearts," "Poetry of the Physical," an implicit denial that the *mind* is involved.

Thus has the classical picture presented by art historians depicted the trajectory of fine art as linear and evolutionary. It parallels the erroneous theory by which social scientists used to trace the development of humanity through several stages to "civilization." Currently post-modernists and feminist art historians are deconstructing many of the most cherished assumptions of art history and aesthetics in order to achieve a more balanced view (Parker and Pollock 1981; Wolff 1983).[2]

I hope those comments clarify some of the issues addressed in these essays. I certainly sanction "meddling" with theory and ideas. Not to be so engaged would entail capitulating to the attitudes that have excluded craft from art theory. However, I disagree with the terminology and categories of art critics. Classical art historical discourse is in drastic need of revision. That is why I do not sanction the division suggested by Foucault, and I hope what I have just said explains why. The spaces that Foucault describes are cultural constructions inscribed through language, and they reflect one of the fundamental premises of linguistic models, that based upon binary oppositions. Paul Mathieu's paper is infused with the experiential, but he draws upon Foucault, who juxtaposes utopias and distopias along the conceptual fault lines drawn to distinguish art from craft. As seductive as a Foucauldian analysis appears to be, I opt for discovering and elaborating upon the roots of this bifurcation rather than capitulating to it. As Joan Vastokas (1992) reminds us, "the legacy of this evolutionary and hierarchical preoccupation with 'lower' and 'higher' forms of human endeavor has become so embedded in Western thought processes that it persists even today as an aspect of the Western world view." Thus the deconstruction of the distinction

2 For a particularly penetrating analysis of the appropriation of indigenous expressive forms by visual artists, see "Sone General Observations on the Problem of Cultural Colonialism" by Kenneth Coutts-Smith in *The Myth of Primitivism: Perspectives on Art,* ed. by Susan Miller (London: Routledge, 1991).

between art and craft aids in dismantling a portion of the "grand legitimizing narrative" (Lyotard 1952)) that provided the hegemonic framework for the triumph of modernism.

We live in a materialistic society which values not only objects over people but creations by dead craftspersons over those contemporary artisans. Paul Mathieu comments on this, and Michele Hardy reflects on the devaluation of tacit knowledge in Western societies. The ascendence of aesthetics as a branch of philosophy privileged the conceptual and provided the justification for the devaluation of experiential, body knowledge. Michele Hardy favours a feminist and reflexive perspective, and it is feminists who have made major contributions in deconstructing the andro- and Eurocentric assumptions that have acted to underpin analytic frameworks for centuries.

I do not look upon crafts as objects only. They *are* objects (we give them names), but I see them primarily as material manifestations of relationships. Making, regardless of the medium, involves tacit knowledge, which is unconscious, implicit, intuitive, and analogical. Makers are as much concerned with process as end product. Creating entails a long process which may involve the maker, family, friends, co-workers, and environmental and spiritual concerns. As Hardy notes, her way of working involves an *awareness of connections,* and craft making becomes a primary means of knowing the world. Given the power, pervasiveness, and persuasiveness of classical art history, aesthetics and science, all of which privilege the *conceptual,* it is not surprising that her experiential knowledge is marginalized and discounted within the halls of academe.

Because craft making is based primarily on "non-verbal" knowledge, it is grounded in the sensuous. This "feeling" is discounted by many semioticians who continue to privilege language as the primary form of communication. Most semiotic analysis borrows heavily from linguistics, and these models have come to serve as the dominant paradigm for the critical interpretation of expressive forms in the post-modern period. But verbal language is inadequate to the task of replicating, communicating, and interpreting all forms of sensate experience (Vastokas 1992). As Wilden (1981, 10) reminds us, "language is one type of communication and one type of semiotic activity. Although the analysis of language provides us with insights into communication, it is generally agreed that language cannot legitimately serve as a general model of communication or semiotics."

Communication involves signification, which is the total impression of the object *without* compartmentalization. Whenever the sign is split into signifier and signified, we are in the realm of language, which is only one form of communication. Of course we need language to talk about various forms of cultural expression, but it is inappropriate to use methods implicitly or explicitly grounded in linguistics to analyse them.[3]

Linguistic approaches to meaning miss the scale of the world in which meaning operates. Craft making can be located squarely within this "arena" because all expressive forms, regardless of the medium, are non-linguistic forms of communication. Communicative forms ought to be examined in a communicative way and not reduced to analyses suitable only for linguistics. Semioticians confuse matter and information. The description of an object is different from the object itself – the map is not the territory: it is a representation of it. The sign, once imposed does *not* come from the object, but emerges from a *produced knowledge outside of it.* The Cross is an object, but it cannot be meaningful without the *context;* nor can it possess qualities without the knower.[4] Sensuous effects are never in the form: they are culturally conceived. Matter is always *located* in form; there is a co-dependency; all objects have both.

A person who takes materials from the natural world and creatively transforms them into a personal expression knows a communion with the environment that totally eludes the participant in modern industrial production. The art critic Suzi Gablik (1987, 31) notes that the deeper aesthetic issue is, "not whether a form is good or bad, but whether it does what it is meant to do at a particular stage of culture's development: nothing is more effective and transformative than a creative activity that fulfills a cultural need."

Gablik's statement demonstrates that the desire to create transcends time and location. It is a natural human impulse, not bound by medium. Classical-art historians and aestheticians need to wake up and smell the coffee (preferably served in a hand-thrown mug). To continue to support outdated dualisms is counter-productive and serves the privileged status quo at the expense of the general population. This insidious bifurcation has dominated long enough. If the hegemonic powers that be concede to a reflexive approach, they will climb down from their ivory towers and humbly acknowledge that the classical perspective should go the way of the dinosaurs.

3 See Anthony Wilden, *System and Structure* (London: Tavistock, 1972), for further elaboration. Wilden is well situated to critique the over-emphasis on linguistic models in semiotics, for he was a student of the famous linguist Roman Jakobson while he was at the Massachusetts Institute of Technology. He also was the first person to translate Laçan's work into English.

4 What "meaning" would the Cross have for a practising Buddhist who had no knowledge of Christianity?

References

Clark, Kenneth. 1967. *Leonardo da Vinci*. Baltimore: Penguin.

Gablik, Suzi. 1987. "The Re-enchantment of Art." *New Art Examiner,* December: 30-32.

Hauser, Arnold. 1965. *Mannerism: The Crisis of the Renaissance and the Origin of Modern Art.* New York: Knopf.

Kant, Immanuel. 1951. *The Critique of Judgement*. New York: Hafner.

Kristeller, Paul O. 1951. "The Modern System of the Arts: A Study in the History of Aesthetics" (I). *Journal of the History of Ideas* 12: 496-527.

– – – 1952. "The Modern System of the Arts: A Study in the History of Aesthetics" (II). *Journal of the History of Ideas* 13: 17-46.

Lyotard, Jean François. 1952. *The Post-modern Condition: A Report on Knowledge*. Theory and History of Literature, Vol. 10. Minneapolis: University of Minnesota Press.

M'Closkey, Kathy. 1985. "The Institutionalization of Art among Two Internal Colonies: A Comparison of the Inuit and the Navajo." M.A. thesis, Department of Sociology, University of Windsor.

Parker, Rozika. 1986. *The Subversive Stitch*. London: Women's Press.

Parker, Rozika, and Griselda Pollock. 1981. *Old Mistresses: Women, Art and Ideology*. New York: Pantheon.

Pevsner, Nikolaus. 1940. *Academies of Art, Past, Present and Future*. Cambridge: University Press.

Sohn-Rethel, Alfred. 1977. *Intellectual and Manual Labor: A Critique of Epistemology*. Atlantic Highlands: Humanities Press.

Thompson, E.P. 1980. *The Making of the English Working Class*. London: Penguin.

Vastokas, Joan. 1992. *Beyond the Artifact: Native Art as Performance*. Toronto: Robart Centre for Canadian Studies.

Wilden, Anthony. 1981. "Semiotics as Praxis: Strategy and Tactics." *Semiotic Inquiry* 1: 1-33.

Wolf, Eric. *Europe and the People without History*. Berkeley: University of California Press, 1982.

Wolff, Janet. 1983. *Aesthetics and the Sociology of Art*. London: George Allen and Unwin.

Historical Contexts

and Contemporary Concerns

DianeSullivanVirginiaWrightJacquesGiardHowardCollinson

Diane E. Sullivan

Decoration and Ornament in Ceramic Art

Diane E. Sullivan is a Canadian

ceramist and an MFA candidate at the

University of Washington in Seattle.

Décoration et ornement : un langage esthétique

Cet exposé analyse les théories de compréhension de la décoration par l'analyse critique des oeuvres de céramique canadiennes contemporaines.

Dans les années 70, le monde artistique occidental fut témoin d'un regain d'intérêt pour la valeur de la décoration en tant que langage esthétique légitime et nouveau. Issu de la popularisation et de la démocratisation culturelle des années 60, la décoration a été perçue comme un art de masse par les artistes et les critiques. Les critiques d'art telles que Amy Goldin ont publié des théories sur la décoration et l'ornementation qui avaient été oubliées depuis que le modernisme avait dominé le monde artistique. Ces théories proclamaient que la décoration pouvait constituer un vide intellectuel sans être stupide. Des discussions subséquentes menées par des théoriciens de l'art sur la création de motifs et les systèmes de décoration de l'Islam continuent d'analyser la pertinence de la compréhension et de l'appréciation de la décoration non pas comme l'un des beaux-arts, mais comme un des arts décoratifs qui a renoncé à la condescendance du monde des beaux-arts et comme symptôme du développement postmoderne

.Les conséquences de cet intérêt renouvelé pour la décoration, l'ornement en artisanat et particulièrement pour la céramique ont été un prestige grandissant dans le monde des arts, prestige fondé sur leur valeur intrinsèque et traditionnelle. Soudainement, l'expression «décoratif» n'était plus péjoratif et les artistes se sont tourné vers la longue tradition de décoration dans les métiers d'art pour y puiser leur inspiration. Dans le monde de l'artisanat, la décoration a fait l'objet d'attaques dans les années 50 et 60 produisant des artistes d'avant-garde tels que Peter Voulkos et Robert Arneson qui se sont concentrés sur l'aspect décoratif, l'ont nié, détruit et ridiculisé avant de le personnaliser et de le transformer en l'un des beaux-arts. Le monde des beaux-arts a à l'heure actuelle reconnu des éléments de l'art décoratif et tente de comprendre son impact sur l'appréciation esthétique. Dans le cas de l'artisanat, la notion du décoratif faisait partie de sa tradition pour plusieurs, et les deux dernières décennies ont amené les historiens de l'art, les critiques d'art et les théoriciens de l'art à perfectionner leur appréciation du langage de la décoration.

A discussion of decoration and ornament within the ceramic-art world is a discussion of a visual language of aesthetics. This discussion must recognize the many influential paradigms that the current ceramics community works within. The ceramist of today crosses many definitions of craft and art, traditional and avant-garde, modern and post-modern; however, within these larger paradigms many use the language of decoration, a language which carries with it its own preconditions, meanings and expectations.

In the 1970s the Western art world witnessed a revival of interest in the value of decoration as a legitimate and alternative language of aesthetics. As an outgrowth of the populist culture of the 1960s, decoration was embraced by fine artists and art critics as art for the masses. Suddenly, the term "decorative" was no longer pejorative. Many artists looked to the long tradition of decoration in the crafts for inspiration. The fine-art world recognized elements of the decorative and attempted to understand its influence on aesthetic appreciation. For modern crafts, which had not clearly defined their own theories of aesthetics, the discourse surrounding this movement, which became known as the "pattern and decoration movement" in painting, provides a strong reference point. Indeed, many ceramists of the seventies, among them Andrea Gill and Joyce Kozloff, began as painters.

It was in connection with a retrospective exhibition of work by Henri Matisse in 1975 that the art critic Amy Goldin published her theories of decoration and proclaimed that decoration may be intellectually empty but need not be stupid. In her further theories of patterning and Islamic systems of decoration, she continued to investigate the relevance of understanding and appreciating decoration, not as fine art, but as decorative art that disclaimed the established art world's condescension. With the growth and rise of post-modernism through the seventies and eighties, work employing decoration and ornamentation increased, as post-modernism fostered a renewed interest in indigenous and varied expression.

Walter Ostrom's work embraces the significance of decoration, and his twenty years teaching at the Nova Scotia College of Art and Design in Halifax have influenced a generation of Canadian ceramists. In the late seventies Ostrom began exploring maiolica glaze decoration over the local Nova Scotian earthenware and has continued this pursuit with greater and greater refinement. His recent work has concentrated on flower bricks, vessels with latticed tops for displaying blooms and foliage.

The concept of the flower brick reflects the relevance of decoration as put forth by Amy Goldin (1975a, 49) in her article on Henri Matisse's use of decoration: decoration does not imply any aim other than beauty, pleasure or the delight of the senses. It is imbued with the immediacy of the present moment, being seen here and now. Images used in decoration have become ritualized and are read by the viewer as given; conceptually they are bland, acting instead as motifs, unchallenging to the constancy of the moment. In the case of the flower brick, this ephemeral quality is accentuated by the introduction and disassemblage of the floral display. When the display is present, the floral motifs on the sides of the bricks act as a frame or support system; when it is absent, they become recognized objects, stimulating the viewer to contemplation. Unlike fine art, decorative art is not intellectualized or personalized: instead it uses motifs that appear to be commonplace and banal (Goldin 1975a, 49). This is a different expression of art from the aesthetic of the drama of the self and human existence or ego. In the case of Ostrom's bricks, the decoration motifs refer to historical ceramics, or the tradition within which the object exists, reinforcing the traditional role of ceramic and decorative art in our culture.

A comment should be made about the difference between ceramic decoration and ceramics as decorative art. Ceramic decoration consists of those elements which combine to achieve a decorative effect. Elements of decoration, therefore, may be used in a work of art without there being a decorative effect, and something may be called decorative which is barren of decoration. The one does not preclude the other; however, an awareness of the difference of the two can assist in an effective reading of the piece.

Spoon and Birds, 1991
by Neil Forrest
ceramic

Tortoise Flowerbrick, 1990
by Walter Ostrom
ceramic
Credit: Elaine Dacey

M Pour Marie Teapot, 1990
by Jeannot Blackburn
ceramic

Ostrom's tortoise bricks (a flower brick in the shape of a tortoise, with the shell as a tile) use elements of Persian decoration; the latticing aspect, while mimicking the pattern on a tortoise shell, is reminiscent of Persian tiles in its specifically hexagonal shape, the application of brilliant colours on a white maiolica base, and the absence of representational motifs. The continuity of the hexagonal shape and application of colours over the surface of the brick challenges the lifelike shape, itself reminiscent of pre-Columbian ware, and forces the viewer to scan the surface in appreciation of the repetitive movement of the decoration.

Decoration evokes a different mode of perception and a different kind of aesthetic experience. The focus is outward: the object reaches out and connects with other kinds of things and situations; it speaks of things common to us all and is, therefore, depersonalized. Its role is one of mediator. This is contradictory to much of our Western fine-art practice, which is inward, personalized and predominantly motivated by intellectual and emotional experiences.

This notion of mediation as a significant function for the language of decoration and ornament was discussed recently in a series of lectures by Oleg Grabar (1992,5) delivered at the National Gallery of Art in Washington, D.C.:

> "The visual order... called ornament... as an initial definition, is differentiated from decoration in the sense that decoration is anything... applied to an object or building, whereas ornament is that aspect of decoration which appears not to have another purpose but to enhance its carrier."

Greg Payce's current work from Calgary is directly influenced by historical sources. What have been called the "post-Minoan" pots use as a reference the ceramic ware of Minoan Crete of the second millennium B.C., employing seafaring creatures that originally were images of regeneration for the Minoan culture. The emphasis of these modern vessels is their function as decorative utilitarian vessels. The surface presents layers of motifs, overlapping and creating a sense of visual depth on the two-dimensional surface and evoking the sense of time that has passed since these motifs were first painted. The handles act as pure ornament to the decoration. Enunciating the more exciting side to the sensory approach to ornament, these vessels are a proclamation of joyful forms endowed with the gift of giving pleasure. They imply that decorative forms are alive, that they breathe more easily than ponderous statues and endless Madonnas (Graber 1992, 40).

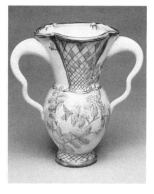

Wild Rose Vase, 1992
by Jim Smith
ceramic
Credit: George Georgakakos

Garniture #2 (night), 1992-3
by Paul Mathieu
ceramic

Detail of Passage, 1993
by Diane Sullivan
ceramic

Neil Forrest's work explores the potential of decoration and ornament through architectural references rather than the vessel tradition. We can analyse Forrest's work for the formal aesthetics of decoration. Formal units of decoration are fields and frames, and it is the relationship between the two which creates the interest for the viewer (Goldin 1975a, 51). The field is the two-dimensional surface or plane of pattern. It reads as a single unit based on a grid. Artistic integrity is equally distributed through the surface. The pattern denies the focus of the classical Renaissance composition: "Pattern is antithetical to the iconic image, for the nature of pattern implicitly denies the importance of singularity, purity, and absolute precision" (Goldin 1975b).

Patterns create a scanning by the viewer, a search for meaning, for truth. The frame acts as a boundary for this process as well as a mediator with the environment and viewer. In Islamic culture patterns were used extensively because Islamic religious doctrines forbade the iconic representation of reality. There too was a visual language that crossed cultural barriers through a consistent application of decorative concepts.

Forrest uses a brilliant colour palette in his work. He inlays motifs of Egyptian paste at regular intervals, in some instances varying the motif itself, in others altering the colour scheme and relying on the motif to create the visual repetition. But what is actual patterning? True, it is presented on a field and is surrounded by a frame, but actual patterning is the repetition of the space between motifs. The unifying factor among the patterns in Forrest's work is the spacing of motifs, which evokes "the presence of hidden laws and an infinity of legitimate unexpressed possibilities" (Goldin 1975b). Forrest then frames these entablatures of pattern with modelled, three-dimensional ornamentation, in this way establishing tension between the notion of Renaissance focus and the non-specificity of decorative patterning.

For the studio ceramist working with tableware, the challenge becomes the relationship between the fabrication of the forms and the decoration of the surface. The Nova Scotian potter Jim Smith has been creating tableware that continues to explore the relationship of pattern and decorative motifs to the form of the vessel. In Smith's work, a handle, a rim, a foot become visual frames for the decoration as well as an evocation of form. The lid of a coffee pot mimics in three dimensions the pattern motif on the body. A luscious handle on a soup tureen repeats the flourish of a sgraffito line of decoration. These elements of framing act as mediators between the decorative surface and the viewer's environment. These boundaries intensify the viewer's awareness of physical space, of the here and now; but it is a public and social space, not the private and intimate one of the Renaissance tradition (Goldin 1975a, 57). As decorative tableware, Smith's work carries the viewer's contemplation of pattern into the surrounding environment, creating, as Matisse would say, a harmonious whole.

The Montreal ceramist Paul Mathieu uses the reference of the frame and field to create the ultimate search by the viewer. In his stacking dinner set *The Arrows of Time,* the multiplicity of the three-dimensional objects is denied by the continuous field of decoration, and the frame is established by rendered line. As one unstacks the dinner set, the three-dimensional motif, the teapot and cup, becomes the subject of the two-dimensional motif, and the time which has passed in the unstacking has satisfyingly been matched by the completion of the cup of tea being served on the flat plane.

On Mathieu's recent garniture sets, fields of decoration overlap on five three-dimensional objects, denying their three-dimensionality; visually the objects are subservient to the surface decoration. The frames that do occur are not based explicitly on the forms but are independent of them. The line is used to frame two-dimensional representations of three-dimensional forms, in this case a male nude pictured at night on one side, and in the day on the other. A play in itself on the historical acceptability of the female nude as a decorative motif, the image of the male nude lies fractured in a decorative morass of vegetal fecundity. A questioning of relationships occurs on the part of the viewer: surface to object, object to environment.

Mathieu's work exists on many levels, as does much decoration and ornamentation. In many cultures it is tacitly understood that to decorate something is to bring beauty or perfection to whatever one adorns and to bring pleasure to the viewer. It only follows that morality is never far from beauty or pleasure. Platonic ideals led to the conclusion that in beauty one finds truth and goodness. We saw this with Ostrom's and Smith's work, which affirmed the beauty of the environment in which we existed; it affirmed our space and confirmed our pleasurable existence. Mathieu exposes these expectations and comments on our culture's preoccupations with the delineation of private and public issues in the stacking dinner set *The Moral Secret of Immorality.* Here the depiction of aroused male genitalia is revealed in the unstacking of a cup painted with a sign of denial. Mathieu is using the expectations surrounding decorated dinnerware in our culture to comment on one of its weaknesses.

Two men who explored the use of ceramics in primitive cultures, Michael Cardew and Harry Davis, recognized that patterning and decoration are integrally linked to the expression of the intuitive, creative self. While in Africa, both men observed that the more primitive tribes decorated their pots with greater diligence when not hindered by market pressure (Davis 1978). Perhaps this can help explain Goldin's (1975a, 49) statement that decoration is a rejection of the dichotomy between nature and culture. It is the synthesizer of cultural manifestations in the realm of nature. It is easy to see why ceramists would embrace such approaches to decoration, since ceramics itself involves the transformation of nature (clay) to culture (the pot).

The west coast producer, Nancy Walker, embraces this intuitive metaphysical search in her work. Her bowls are often pinched, and decorated with burnished slips. They incorporate the three-dimensional re-creation of the two-dimensional decorative motif balancing on the rim. This piece, entitled *Hello?* is from the series *Women on the Edge*. The vessel as symbol of the female body is an age-old one, and Walker uses it with a poetic sensitivity. In *Riding Around,* also part of the *Women on the Edge* series, the rim ornaments help determine a balance for the bowl, which rocks without a definite place to rest. Women helping each other find a place to rest. To the viewer's amusement, the women ride the rim of the bowl, which is decorated with the horses they may one day connect with.

For many, decoration and ornamentation have been identified not only with the intuitive, but also with the feminine. Similarly, much has been written about the feminine quality of the crafts, the crafts being inherently decorative, in their traditional pleasure-seeking role in the world of visual production. This view has been alternately denied and applauded, depending on one's political views. Lending weight to the notion of a feminine language of decoration are the recent publications by the archaeo-mythologist Marija Gimbutas (1989), specifically *The Language of the Goddess,* which addresses the prehistoric development of many of the old European decorative motifs, still in use today, and argues that they are directly related to the worship of an all-encompassing Earth Mother, who is also manifested in the form of the bird and snake goddess. Decoration which once seemed arbitrary is shown to be a highly developed language of contemplation surrounding rebirth, regeneration, and fertility. Chevrons, or V's, were schematized bird feet, coils were snakes, the life energy, symbols of regeneration. Leaf shapes were vulvas, a source of feminine power. The meander, or fret, was schematized water, the source of life.

Laurie Rolland's sense of decoration contemporizes these earlier motifs on chalice-like vessels, designed to be appreciated in a frontal manner like a human body. On *Bird/Figure Vessel,* the decoration is repeated in the form, and the long neck of the vase itself appears as a long birth canal. *Winged Vessel* engages the spiral motif amidst water lines and refers to the passage of the physical to the spiritual world, a theme found in much primitive decoration.

Many ceramists use the vessel as an archetypal motif, a fundamental prop or symbol of civilization. Vessels are basic, timeless. The visual producer Jeannie Mah, of Regina, has focused on the historic vessel for her expression. This reference is evident in such titles as *Sevres Teapot* and *Sevres Teacup.* The cup in Mah's work has become the banal motif; it is not a representation of anything else. It is a very self-conscious cup and has become an image, a parody, of itself. This tension and self-awareness are extended through the application of a surface decoration that implies a continuity of space, the pattern establishing a constancy that imparts the irrelevance of perfect form. The razor-sharp lip, decorative swirl handle, and disassociated pedestal foot frame a surface that becomes dimensionally ambiguous since the pattern implies a continuation beyond the form. The essential timelessness of this archetypal image is enunciated through the application of a decoration that appears to be a fragment of a stellar pattern. There is in Mah's work a criticism of the world this cup comes from. To quote Mah (1992), "The Cup, as a symbol of sustenance contorts itself to conform to a role of social acceptability, appearing in formal dress, as an object of desire."

Jeannot Blackburn's teapots also offer a criticism of the culture within which they are produced. Excessively ornate, the teapots consist of an assemblage of Barbie-doll-like limbs, red-lipped heads, and ornately stylized letters, the colours acidly commercial. In *D pour Delores* and *M pour Marie,* the female form has become the teapot, an object of mass production and desire. In *M pour Marie* the head is contorted between the menacingly aggrandized letter M, while a brilliant yellow high-heeled shoe foolishly tilts off the tip of the spout. Oleg Grabar (1992, 45) has written:

> Ornament is itself or exhibits most forcefully an intermediate order between viewers and users of art, perhaps even creators of art and works of art. This intermediate spirit takes many forms, but all of them are characterized by one central feature: while necessary to the comprehension of a work of art, they are not, except in a few extreme cases, the work of art itself... they are what some literary critics have called the prisms mediating between the world and the text or the text and its readers.

For Blackburn the text is the commentary on our society's commodification of humanity; the use of ornament delivers this message to the viewer and, in this case, has transformed the very purpose of the carrier, which is the teapot.

The world of visual production today is a world of immense diversity. It offers the viewer a wide range of aesthetic languages, replete with their respective histories and traditions. For ceramics, as for much of the traditional crafts, the language of decoration and ornament is a language that is closely associated with its origins, and offers the contemporary producer a wealth of avenues of exploration.

References

Davis, Harry. 1978. "An Historical Review of Art, Commerce and Craftmanship." *Studio Potter* 6, no. 1 (1978): 9.

Gimbutas, Marija. 1989. *The Language of the Goddess*. New York: Harper Collins.

Goldin, Amy. 1975a. "Matisse and Decoration: The Shchukin Panels." *Art in America* 63: 49.

Goldin, Amy. 1975b. "Patterns, Grids and Painting." *Artforum,* September: 50.

Grabar, Oleg. 1992. *The Mediation of Ornament*. Princeton, N.J.: Princeton University Press.

Mah, Jeannie. 1992. Artist's statement.

Virginia Wright

Craft Education in Canada:
A History of Confusion

Virginia Wright is a

Toronto design historian, curator,

teacher, and retailer.

L'éducation artisanale au Canada : un passé confus

La signification de l'artisanat contemporain est une conséquence cumulative des actions privées et publiques. Elle constitue dans une certaine mesure la signification imposée par la société à la communauté des artisans, plutôt que celle simplement transmise en sens inverse, sous la forme d'objets finis et de bonnes intentions. La signification de l'artisanat peut être issue de thèmes plus vastes qui soutiennent ou bien pervertissent la valeur intrinsèque du travail artisanal lui-même.

Au Canada, l'histoire de l'artisanat professionnel depuis la première guerre mondiale a été influencée par des événements tels que les expositions universelles, par des thèmes tels que le statut relatif et législatif des institutions d'enseignement et des professions ainsi que par les modes, dans les médias par exemple, et en muséologie.

Ces influences diverses ont largement nui au développement d'une conscience artisanale mûre et confiante au Canada. La communauté artisanale a été tour à tour choyée et violemment critiquée. Par exemple, tous les métiers d'art ont été négativement influencés par la lutte suivant la deuxième guerre mondiale au sujet de l'enseignement de la conception, une lutte non officielle mais vigoureusement menée entre les écoles d'art et les universités ainsi qu'entre les facultés d'ingénierie et d'architecture à l'intérieur des universités, de même qu'entre la vieille garde antiproductrice et la nouvelle garde techniquement téméraire à l'intérieur des programmes de métiers d'art des écoles d'art.

La structure actuelle de l'enseignement de l'artisanat, le statut de l'artisanat et la «signification» de l'artisanat au Canada sont tous manifestement le résultat d'un type d'expérience collective qui survient parallèlement aux efforts individuels pour produire une oeuvre significative sur le plan personnel. Cet exposé retrace ces événements et ces thèmes sur une période de cinquante ans, de 1920 à 1970. Une connaissance plus approfondie de cette histoire publique pourrait contribuer à forger des stratégies nouvelles en vue de la formation et du soutien des artisans professionnels.

The meaning of contemporary craft is the cumulative result of private and public acts. It is, to some extent, a meaning imposed by society on the craft community, not simply conveyed in the other direction in the form of finished objects and good intentions. The significance of craft is determined by its relationship to larger issues, which either support or subvert the intrinsic value of the craft work itself. One of these larger issues is the nature and status of craft education.

The training of craftspeople became institutionalized during the late nineteenth and early-twentieth centuries. Woodworking and metalworking were taught as trades to working-class boys in vocational schools, while other crafts were taught to middle-class students in art schools, where male students favoured jewellery design and wood carving, and female students, pottery and weaving.

The history and theory of the crafts, to the extent that they were taught in the art schools, were minor components of the history of art or the history of ornament. Emphasis was placed on ancient or classical objects, studied when possible in local museum collections. Studio training was referred to as "applied art" or "applied design." The former served to distinguish craft from fine art, while the latter raised the prestige of technical courses that were in many cases reminders of the vocational-school origins of the art schools. At the Ontario College of Art (OCA), for example, which had previously been the Central Ontario School of Art and Industrial Design, the crafts were clearly separated from fine art. The new college's 1919 Act of Incorporation described its purpose as "the training of students in the fine arts, including drawing, painting, design, modelling and sculpture, and in all branches of the applied arts in the more artistic trades and manufactures."

In the 1920s every second-year student in the Department of Design and Applied Art at OCA was required to do bench work in stained glass, woodwork, metalwork, and pottery. (Their first year had consisted mainly of exer-

Woman at kiln,
Ontario College of Art,
Toronto, 1954

cises in geometry and stencilling.) Third- and fourth-year students could then specialize in jewellery and enamelling, stained glass, or pottery and ceramics. These studio activities were variously referred to in the college's 1929 prospectus as "design," "industrial design," "applied art," "applied design," "industrial art," and "craft."

This variety of names reveals a high degree of institutional confusion. The crafts, though recognized as skilled professional disciplines in Europe and the United States, were allowed to languish in Canada as sub-departments of art or technical design, or as part-time hobby courses. Craft teachers were denied independent departmental status, and when institutions juggled their priorities, as they often do, craft programs were left to fall where they might.

In most cases they became simply practical courses to provide workbench experience for students in vaguely defined design departments. This was their status until the Second World War, when the pace of industrial research and development relegated the crafts to an even lower rung on the academic ladder. Craft traditions and craft education were seen to be considerably less interesting and less important than the training of designers for industry. At the Ontario College of Art this banishment from the higher realms of both art and design was signalled by a new, painfully modest collective name for craft courses: "manual industry." Crafts in Canada were firmly pegged as a minor component of post-war manufacturing. The crafts enjoyed a brief moment of government support and funding at the end of the war, when they were widely promoted for their supposed therapeutic value. Craft activities were organized for new community centres and were enthusiastically promoted for the rehabilitation of returned servicemen and women. Woodworking and weaving, in particular, were recommended for calming the nerves and rebuilding self-confidence. The Ontario College of Art added occupational therapy to its list of courses.

Whilst enhancing the appreciation of craft among the public, these rehabilitation programs contributed little to the development of professional craft disciplines in Canada. In many schools, the crafts were now required to straddle three entirely different sets of objectives. In 1945, F.S. Haines (1945, 207), the president of OCA, described the three "priorities" for the crafts: firstly, developing designers for the various crafts; secondly, training craft teachers for high schools and vocational schools; thirdly, encouraging adults to take up handicrafts as hobbies. This mixed mandate did little more than serve the limited needs of local industries and school boards. The deliberate promotion of amateur crafts, in particular, was very damaging to the public's view of professional studio training and practice.

The tentativeness of craft education and the lack of a clear commitment to the independent professional status of the crafts made craft education vulnerable to the anti-craft propaganda of post-war industrial boosters. Donald Buchanan (1945), one of the founding editors of *Canadian Art* magazine and an influential advocate of industrial design and mass production, sarcastically described the craft program at the Ontario College of Art as "patterns for wallpapers and textiles, lettering, leatherwork, and wood-carving." He insisted that these types of courses "must be definitely demarcated from the more advanced technical and organizational understanding that must be given students who want to specialize in designing for machine production." In other words, the teaching of design, which was more "advanced" should be cut off from the teaching of crafts, which apparently were less "advanced."

Having been press-moulded into pale imitations of industrial designers, craft students and teachers now found themselves consigned to academic limbo at the very moment when the work of professional craftspeople in Canada was showing promise of a new maturity and when the crafts community as a whole could have benefited greatly from clearly focused institutional support.

Real design and industry were seen to be the territory of the boys with the toys, who would use industrial processes developed during the war to promote new products, new industries, and new profits. At the time, the business potential seemed huge because Canada had emerged from the war as the world's third-largest exporter of manufactured goods. This unprecedented status was due, of course, to the severely weakened state of the European economies and, as it turned out, could not be sustained. For a number of years, however, there were very high expectations and an ambitious program of industrial design research and development. Industrial design was the focus of all government design advocacy, of which there was a considerable amount (most of it orchestrated by Donald Buchanan). Engineering and architecture faculties across the country competed with the art schools and with each other to introduce new industrial design courses.

Any interest in the subject from other quarters, especially the crafts, was actively discouraged. This was forcefully demonstrated by Buchanan's response to an exhibition called *Design in Industry,* which was organized by the Ontario section of the Canadian Handicraft Guild, along with the Royal Ontario Museum, in the summer of 1945. The exhibition included fine craft and industrial products from Canada and other countries, installed in gracious, realistic settings so as to enhance the interplay of the handmade with the machine-made. And the work was all functional, to emphasize the message to manufacturers that Canadian craftspeople had significant potential as designers of mass-produced household goods. A report on the exhibition in *Canadian Homes and Gardens* (June 1945) said that the exhibition would "make Canadians conscious of the design possibilities of their own materials" and "inspire and stimulate the study and application of original design in Canada." It concluded that the exhibition would "show the place of the designer craftsman in successful industrial production."

Buchanan was not impressed. He attacked the exhibition with a feature article in *Canadian Art,* saying that the name of the exhibition, *Design in Industry,* was a "misnomer" and that the exhibition only proved that "in Canada, the promotion of art in industry has a long way yet to go." Specifically, he thought that the Canadian woodwork in the exhibition was "adolescent," that the glass making needed "more criticism," and that the furniture was "weak." He accused the exhibition organizers of ignoring what he thought was the really important issue: what new products could be made with "aluminum sheets, magnesium rods, plywood, chemical plastics and cellulose compounds?" (Buchanan 1945, 195).

What Buchanan and other Canadian industrial design advocates chose not to acknowledge was that surface design, graphic design, fine woodworking, in fact all the crafts, had significant potential connections to machine production. He chose not to discuss the influence of the crafts on product design and seemed to be unaware of the complex historical relationship between the two. Buchanan's writing was criticized on this point by a reader, Deane Russell (1945, 44) of Ottawa, who wrote to *Canadian Art,* signing himself as "Secretary, Interdepartmental Committee on Arts and Crafts." Russell reported a "widely shared feeling of exception" to Buchanan's statement that the application of new materials to household uses had "more potential value" than the "encouragement of very minor crafts such as wood carving by amateur craftsmen." Russell pointed out that in Sweden promoters of industrial design recognized that "their efforts would be incomplete unless comparable efforts were made to encourage the people themselves to participate in design and craft programs on a national scale." He warned that "industrial arts should not be promoted to the exclusion of other creative art and craft interests."

At that time it was estimated that there were about sixty thousand looms and one hundred thousand spinning wheels in use in Quebec alone. This was mentioned in the British magazine *The Studio* (Brieger 1945). The quality of the work was said to be "outstanding." According to the writer, the standard of textiles and hooked rugs from Quebec and the Maritime provinces was higher than that of any comparable Canadian machine-made products. In furniture, too, he thought that the work of "individual cabinet makers" was "far in advance of that of large manufacturers."

So the outsider status of crafts in the schools was not due to any deficiency in either the quantity or quality of the craftwork actually being done in many parts of the country. It was due, as the Montreal weaver Karen Bulow said, to the lack of "support from the government, universities and the public" (Buchanan 1949, 54). This lack of support was most evident in the art schools, which processed craft students without giving them any independent departmental recognition, and in the universities, which ignored professional craft disciplines completely.

The situation has changed little since then in most parts of the country and has been exacerbated by the tendency of craft associations in Canada to promote amateur craft activities at the expense of more rigorous professional practice. Very few schools or departments have the word "craft" where it really matters – in their official titles, on their letterheads, over their front doors. The crafts are still in the Canadian educational closet, confused about their right to a distinct academic and professional identity – an identity clearly delineated by their own history, their own technologies, their own critical language, and their own cultural and educational objectives.

References

Brieger, Peter. 1945. "Handicrafts and Industrial Design." *The Studio*, April.

Buchanan, D. 1945. "Design in Industry – A Misnomer." *Canadian Art*, Summer.

– – – 1949. "Fine Craftsmanship and Mass Production." *Canadian Art*, Christmas.

Canadian Homes and Gardens. 1945. "Does Contemporary Design Mean Anything to You?" *Canadian Homes and Gardens*, June.

Haines, F.S. 1945. "A New School of Design." *Canadian Art*, Summer.

Russell, Deane. 1945. "Correspondence." *Canadian Art*, November.

Jacques Giard

Contemporary Industrial Design:
Is There a Place for Crafts?

Jacques Giard is Director

of the School of Industrial Design at

Carleton University in Ottawa.

Le design industriel contemporain :
les «arts appliqués» y ont-ils leur place?

On peut retracer les origines du design industriel à cette période de l'histoire où le geste créateur de l'artisan devait s'imprégner des impératifs de la production industrielle. Avec le temps, ce qui s'avérait être un travail artisanal utilitaire, mais néanmoins personnel, devint, par la force des choses, plus impersonnel, plus fade, du fait de l'industrialisation galopante. Et s'il y eut à une certaine époque un lien étroit entre l'artisan et le designer industriel, les années écoulées ont tôt fait d'effacer presque totalement ces liens ancestraux.

Cependant, que penser du design industriel contemporain? Est-ce que le postmodernisme et sa mission de libération artistique ont modifié l'échiquier pour les designers?

La remise en question de toute la doctrine moderniste a-t-elle émancipé le designer industriel de sorte qu'il manifeste à nouveau le goût de côtoyer, de visiter certains aspects des «arts appliqués» laissés pour compte depuis bien des années? Les artisans, pour leur part, ont-ils un rôle prépondérant à jouer dans la conception et la fabrication des objets usuels industriellement produits ou l'industrie considère-t-elle toujours que «arts appliqués» et artisanat sont incompatibles? Quelles sont les implications, en matière d'éthique, sur les plans social et professionnel que l'on doit considérer dans ce débat, cette ré-évaluation qui touchent à la fois les designers et les artisans?

Dans cette communication, l'auteur, designer industriel et directeur d'une des plus importantes écoles de design industriel au Canada, se propose de situer le design industriel dans son contexte historique (surtout en ce qui touche ses racines dans les divers «arts appliqués») et de retracer son évolution en regard des innombrables contributions à l'essor de certaines industries tant au Canada qu'à travers le monde. L'auteur proposera également des scénarios possibles pour l'avenir du design industriel et tout spécialement sa réconciliation avec les «arts appliqués».

Introduction

Early in my career, I had the opportunity to work with Ian Bruce, the designer and builder of the Laser sailboat. Aside from the fact that it was a memorable experience in an even more memorable time – Canada, after Expo 67 – I was doing precisely what I thought industrial designers should be doing, that is, designing products to better meet the needs of the user. And for me, the focus of my attention at the time – the Laser sailboat – was a nearly perfect example of good industrial design. Not only was it an innovative and creative idea, but the Laser was produced in large quantities so that many people could enjoy it.

At one point during those years, Bruce met the painter Alex Colville, who happened to be in Montreal for a gallery opening of his recent works. The evening was progressing as such evenings usually do: people mingling, talking, and generally socializing. At one point, however, Colville approached Bruce and unexpectedly asked if he had any interest in buying a painting in which the Laser appeared. Without too much hesitation, Bruce replied that he would no more buy the original painting than sell the original Laser. Instead, Bruce said kindly, he preferred to wait for a print signed by the artist. Like so many industrial designers, Bruce believed that the availability of many copies was more important than the uniqueness of the original.

Before this anecdote labels me as a Philistine, please allow me to provide a context for my story. I do not mean to suggest that quantity automatically implies quality or, worse, superiority. In fact, I would argue that, with few exceptions, there is little if any correlation between quantity and quality. If nothing else, popular taste will lay that proposition to rest.

But thinking now about the discussion that ensued between Ian Bruce and Alex Colville, it is clear that one aspect of the reigning premise of industrial design was central to Bruce's response. Simply put, this premise states that manufactured products are only the means to an end, not an end in themselves. This view seems to conflict immediately with that of the artist, a view in which the expression of self is often paramount. Placed at opposite ends of a continuum, however, a scale is created which more readily shows our respective professional positions – crafts closer to the self end of the scale and industrial design closer to the user end. The gap between the two is my topic for discussion and the one to be reconciled.

A Short History

Before commenting further on the contemporary schism between industrial design and crafts, I would like to point out some of the characteristics they share – their origins, their nature, and their continued presence. Bringing out the family album can refresh our memories of things forgotten – selectively or otherwise.

Most industrial designers are quite aware that their pedigree can be traced directly back to the crafts. If not immediately obvious, the link is revealed in art or design history courses early in a designer's formal education, articles in design publications, presentations at conferences, and so on. Only the most myopic of industrial designers would deny the historical link between crafts and industrial design.

Probably the most critical period in the relationship between industrial design and crafts was the Industrial Revolution in England. Before that, the craftsperson was more or less the sole agent for the production of everyday objects. With the introduction of mass production, however, everyday objects could be produced mechanically and without the need of skilled craftspeople. Suddenly, the artisan was seen as unnecessary by most if not all manufacturers. Some manufacturers, such as Josiah Wedgewood, did see a role for a new kind of artisan. He continued to call upon the skills of the artisan but within the context of the manufactory, as he called it. So was born industrial design and, with it, the initial parting of the ways.

For most artisans of the day, however, despair overshadowed any possible glimmer of hope for the future. It came as no surprise therefore that certain individuals were to propose a revisionary mandate in hopes of finding those values displaced by the industrial processes. William Morris's activities placed him in the forefront of the people trying to address this contentious issue. Looking at his many design and retail ventures with the hindsight we now have, even successes such as IKEA are nothing really new.

Later, similar insights to those of Morris began to appear in other parts of Europe. For example, at the turn of this century Germany saw artists, craftspeople, designers, architects, and manufacturers unite in a common

Sussex rush-seated settle

W. Morris and Company

Seating, 1982

by Deganello, Italy

cause under the banner of the Deutsches Werkbund. Its mandate was "the ennoblement of industrial labour through the collaboration of art, industry, and crafts in education, propaganda and a united approach to relevant questions." And a few years later – in 1919 to be exact – the Bauhaus was established, a school of design that had its curriculum deeply rooted in arts and crafts. This particular pedagogical direction would prove to be prophetic, for it was to become the most influential school of design of this century.

In more recent times, Scandinavia stands out as one place where the integrity associated with crafts has not always been sacrificed for the sake of mass production. Although there are many examples of this union, the evolution of the Finnish company iittala is rather typical of this Scandinavian model. Begun in 1881 by a Swedish glass blower by the name of Abrahamsson, iittala is now one of the leading glass manufacturers in Scandinavia and continues to involve the leading craftspeople of Finland in designing its products.

In North America, the direction of design – and perhaps crafts – was unfortunately not as enlightened as it was in Europe. It evolved, not from a cultural platform, but as a commercial tool of industry. In most instances, early American industrial designers used their artistic and design abilities to manipulate form and colour as a means of styling a product, the principal purpose being to increase retail sales. Consequently, industrial design became a tool of marketing. And because crafts had a comparatively short history in America, with little if any indigenous base, manufacturers of everyday objects evolved in ways quite different from their counterparts in Europe. The design imperatives exhibited by Olivetti in Italy have never had their equivalents in North America.

As for Canada, its branch–plant economic policy provided even less opportunity for the involvement of designers, let alone craftspeople. In many cases, manufacturing plants were located here and there throughout the country for political expediency or fiscal considerations. To the manufacturers who established themselves here, we were a source of manual labour, not creative skill. Our low record of funding for research and development compared to other G7 countries continues to bear this fact out.

What of Today?

Given this history that industrial designers and craftspeople share, why do we more often than not persist in seeing ourselves as long lost artistic cousins? Why does the gap remain? Why are we not bridging it? Have we retained certain similarities which can bind us together ethically? And can we ever hope to be reunited? I may not have answers to all of these questions but there are some general patterns that I would like to share with you.

First, I must admit that I am not well versed in the current direction of the world of crafts. Speaking from the standpoint of an industrial designer, however, I believe that there are national, international, and global factors that cannot be ignored, especially as they affect the presence of everyday objects. These potential philosophical hurdles certainly concern industrial design, and I would not be surprised to learn that they also apply to crafts. Three of them are of particular interest to me: quality, quantity, and commercialism. All three are important to the very future of the everyday object and, coincidentally, are at the heart of our reconciliation.

Quality

Quality is central to most issues of crafts and design, yet defies definition. The measurement of quality is highly subjective and only occasionally finds common ground for agreement. Industrial designers seek certain values when looking for quality in objects of design. The list is sometimes short but more frequently, long; its specific content at times obvious, at other times not. In general terms, industrial designers associate quality with solutions appropriate to the intended use, or measure it in terms of creative breakthroughs where something never before seen forces us to re-evaluate our attitudes. In a narrower sense, quality in industrial design can be the correct material for the task, or the ideal texture for the surface, or the perfect colour for the purpose. It would seem that even in the era of post-modernism, the Almighty is still in the details.

My favourite anecdote to do with quality and manufactured products is set right here in Ottawa. It seems that a local retailer of Waterford glassware has to explain regularly to some of his customers that crystal drinking glasses which have been individually hand-blown and cut can never be identical. You see, his customers regularly return glasses because, to their deep consternation, they find that no two are exactly alike. It is their belief, I suppose, that if two-dollar glasses at Woolco are all identical then surely fifty-dollar glasses should at least meet this fundamental criterion of quality.

Quantity

Quantity, for its part, is often considered the antithesis of quality, a view not always justified. This view is principally due, I believe, to the fact that people can more readily comprehend the value-neutral nature of quantity than the arbitrariness of quality. The specific value of a number is rarely in doubt; the relativity implied by quality almost always is.

Quantity has a further negative connotation. A very large number of manufactured products – an extremely large number, in fact – is sometimes by its very nature considered inherently bad. We have learned all too well that the quantity of anything is somehow inversely proportional to its quality and subsequently believe that too much of a good thing is a bad thing.

Yet, as we have seen, quantity is synonymous with industrial design. In fact, industrial design without quantity becomes a plausible definition of crafts, albeit a simplistic one. The industrial designer takes a more democratic approach, if you will, to the phenomenon of quantity; if a good idea can help one person, then its multiplication makes it that much better. Designers, as you will remember, see their products only as a means to an end.

Commercialism

Of the three factors – quality, quantity, and commercialism – commercialism is the one that inspires the most fear in the creative community. Commercialism reeks of some undesirable and unspeakable ethos, where the designer, if that name dare be used, is pandering to the wishes of the manufacturer, who, in pursuit of the almighty dollar, is catering in turn to the uneducated taste of the user. If red roses on vases are desired by the people, then who are we to question their taste?

Much like quantity, commercialism is not regarded by the industrial designer in solely negative terms. In this age of product proliferation, the commercialism stigma that is often attached to industrial design is in most instances undeserved. The challenge that often faces industrial designers is similar to the task facing a translator or interpreter. Industrial designers are being asked to take an electronic device offering unheard-of possibilities and translate the vocabulary of engineering into the vernacular of the user. Instead of using words, however, the industrial designer uses the visual language, manipulating it with the same demands of rhetoric, semantics, and pragmatism that are found in linguistics.

Reconciliation: The Possibility is There

From my perspective, the picture for industrial design in Canada for the next decade looks somewhat like this. World trade is removing many of the borders in the import and export of manufactured goods, and this trend will continue. That, of course, has made it much easier for some Canadian manufacturers to amortize the total costs of product development because of the greater market potential. On the other hand, the satisfaction of a larger market usually means a more visually global design or what I call the design of the least offensive. The infamous Big Mac is a perfect example of this non-offensive design. Its popularity is not because it is the best hamburger made anywhere; in fact, it is quite mediocre. It has become popular because we are guaranteed the same quality regardless of where we purchase it. It is this guarantee of a known value that has made the Big Mac successful, not its promise of an epicurean delight.

As gloomy as this forecast may sound, this lack of visual design quality is our first area of possible reconciliation or, at least, our first shared battleground; the antidote to the design of the least offensive is the art of the unique. This particular tack is nothing new and was once shared by both crafts and industrial design in their early days together. The uniqueness of anything creates differentiation from everything else, and even the industrial world has realized this fact. For example, the dogma of modernism, as rational and good as it may have been, was inevitably displaced by the uniqueness of post-modernism because the former became predictable and, subsequently, the least offensive.

Quantity is also a rallying point for industrial design and crafts but for reasons that are just now emerging. Previously, mass production of a product literally meant the largest number of economically justifiable bland products. However, mass production methods are changing dramatically, owing principally to the versatility afforded by computers. What this means is that small runs of more specialized products can now be manufactured with as much ease and at the same reasonable cost of larger runs. No longer do large production runs result automatically in the dilution of visual uniqueness.

Commercialism, the last of our three philosophical hurdles, is also going through some radical re-evaluations. For many of us, the word still conjures up negative images – visions of compromise or artistic prostitution. Coming full circle in our analysis, the commercial position of Canada in the global marketplace will force us to shed our role of visual imitators and assume one of innovators. The uniqueness of design alluded to earlier will clearly have to be part of this strategy. Commercialism may well force us to become leaders in the field of design rather than followers.

Conclusions

The question originally posed was the place of crafts – or, more importantly, the craft ethos – within industrial design. It is my feeling that the creativity and originality of design in crafts cannot and, in fact, should not be ignored by industrial design nor by the traditional user of industrial design services. The visual limitations that once restricted us because of mass-production technology and processes are no longer in play. And neither is the narrow commercial emphasis once imposed by marketing and other business fortune-tellers. Add to this the inadvisability of competing head-on with low-wage countries with our labour-intensive products, and all of a sudden the implied liability of unique designs in limited quantities becomes questionable. Our common ground becomes even more apparent.

I believe that there are three fronts on which we can begin to make progress towards a reconciliation. The central players are the designer, the manufacturer, and the user. And, quite coincidentally, there are three time frames in which this reconciliation can occur: short term for the designer, medium term for the manufacturer, and long term for the user.

Design education is by far the easiest and quickest way to begin the process of change I am talking about. By raising the awareness of the connection between crafts and industrial design, we can begin to influence the output of designers. Speaking with a knowledge of the Ontario post-secondary system only, I know that the schools of industrial design have become totally divorced from the schools of crafts. Our long separation has created misconceptions about our respective positions in the creative process of the everyday object. Yet we have a great deal to share. Maybe it is time to consider a more common curriculum or participate in the same design competitions. Without proposing a detailed plan, I would be interested in hearing ideas about how we could begin the process.

For our part, we in the manufacturing sector may require more time before we can see results, if not in Canada, certainly elsewhere. The VIA (Valorization et innovation dans l'ameublement) program in France is a very good example of how artisans and designers have become actively involved with manufacturers. Over the last ten years, this venture, which is funded equally by the association of furniture manufacturers and the government, has had a significant influence on the quality of French furniture. This has enhanced sales in both its domestic and foreign markets at a time when most economic indicators were forecasting the opposite.

Canada has not seized on this economic opportunity with quite the same resourcefulness but the initiatives of Virtu (a charitable arts organization that supports design) are a step in the right direction. By encouraging young designers and artisans to enter its annual competition, Virtu hopes to invigorate both the manufacturing and retail sectors of the furniture industry. But we still have a long way to go. In a recent survey of its consumers, the furniture manufacturers of Quebec were perturbed to discover that their European-look-alike furniture was not recognized as Quebec-made. And why should it be? The manufacturers had been too successful at their old game of borrowing the designs and styles from everywhere else. To the average consumer, if the furniture looks Italian, then it must be Italian.

Lastly, the consumer must never be left out of the loop. Unfortunately, popular taste has rarely kept pace with the leading edge of design or, I would imagine, of crafts. Although the gap between the shock of the new and its acceptability as the norm is still wide, it is getting smaller. However, our democratic tendencies may have to be tempered for some time yet, forcing us to retain our so-called elitist role. But given that Canadian industry can no longer afford simply to follow trends and is now forced into the position of creating them, it is logical to assume that the products of these industries will have to be unique in form as well as in function.

Viewed more abstractly, our professions are profoundly similar in their internal belief systems but, in the eyes of so many observers, have taken on quite different personae. The particular conditions of the past forced us apart but without ever uprooting us. And now, for equally compelling reasons, we are afforded the opportunity to co-operate and collaborate, to reconcile views that once seemed mutually exclusive. I look forward to the re-union.

Howard Collinson – Respondent

Historical Contexts

and Contemporary Concerns

Howard Collinson is Head of the

Institute for Contemporary Culture at the Royal

Ontario Museum in Toronto. He has

curated numerous exhibitions, including

Truth and Beauty, and Documenting Design.

Résumé

On nous a présenté diverses interprétations de la nature et du rôle des métiers d'art qui tournent en partie autour de la relation entre métiers d'art et design, entre métiers d'art et art. Bien que cette question puisse avoir son importance pour qui pratique un métier d'art, la méthodologie récente de l'histoire de l'art se soucie moins de définir le type d'objet qu'elle étudie. Elle étudie de la même façon les produits de l'art, du design ou des métiers d'art. De plus, si l'on considère son évolution historique depuis trois cents ans, on constate que cette différenciation entre disciplines est une création moderne qui n'est aucunement inhérente aux différents moyens d'expression.

All three of these papers, indeed, much of what is being said at this conference deals with the relation of the current state of craft to its history. Different interpretations of the nature and role of craft have been presented, many of which concentrate on the apparent opposition of craft and art. Whereas Dr. Giard and Ms. Wright examine the relationship of craft and design, Ms. Sullivan has chosen to look to the ideas involved in art. She demonstrates that decoration and ornament partake of an established language. It is at least partly by virtue of its relationship to this language that any abstract ornamental or decorative motif is able to carry meaning.

As has been pointed out by both Ms. Wright and Dr. Giard, this problem of definition is not new. Indeed, if I were to say I was a design historian, what period of time would come to mind? If I were a historian of decorative arts, would you automatically assume I deal with handmade objects, mostly from before 1900? My employer, the European Department of the Royal Ontario Museum, solves this problem by playing it safe and defining our area as decorative arts and design, although we would be hard pressed to define the difference. If we ask ourselves what historic craft might be, how would we define it?

Although Dr. Giard points out that the split between craft and design had occurred by the nineteenth century, I wonder if we can't find incipient elements of the design profession in even earlier periods. Indeed the kind of integration of craft and design being proposed by two of the speakers has been the norm for most of the last four or five centuries. In the process of learning about the decorative arts, I recall being struck by the example of Paul Storr, the great English silversmith of the early nineteenth century. Most people, even knowledgeable silver collectors, speak of Paul Storr silver as if he had made each piece with his own hands. In fact, he had a staff of three hundred people and was not averse to using new mechanical procedures such as electrotyping. Was he a craftsman or a designer?

Throughout the history of what I'll call decorative arts, the relationship of makers to designers is quite varied. Eighteenth-century French furniture might be considered a pinnacle of craft, albeit the work is usually a collaboration of several masters of various skills. However, the men we customarily call the makers frequently did not design the work which bears their name. They executed someone else's design. I would argue that the borders between art, craft, production craft, and design are so imprecise as to make the terms meaningless. But just as contemporary makers and educators, curators and granting agencies are caught up in the word play which locates their activity within a particular discourse, this is reflected in our understanding, or lack of understanding, of the history of made things in general.

However, art history seems to be abandoning its interest in such categorization. There are new modes of interpretation being used which are useful for any type of object and do not differentiate between various fields.

One powerful development has been the influence of Marxist history. All objects, whether paintings or chairs, are examined in terms of their patronage, their markets, and the ideology reflected in their form. The comparatively new field of semiotics need not make any distinction between art and non-art. And the field of art history is being encroached on by material culture studies, which see all objects as historical phenomena.

We have become increasingly aware that painting and sculpture have historically served a function, whether this is to decorate a palace or to affirm the propriety of the divine right of kings. Conversely, we are now more aware that objects of "decorative art," such as furniture and silver, are not just glorified utilitarian objects but have an iconography and meaning. They are no longer studied in a purely antiquarian manner but are interpreted with a subtlety previous reserved for "high art." There may, in fact, be a difference between art and craft. I'm just not sure that I care what it is. I'm not sure it is important for our understanding of the objects.

The comparatively recent split between craft and design has been, as Dr. Giard points out, a function of technologically driven systems of production. While we can probably all envision an expanded collaboration between craft and design in the manufacture of objects in the traditional craft media of wood, glass, ceramic, metal, and textiles, and even in new material when used in the production of simple consumer goods, I wonder where such collaboration might be possible in the manufacture of more complex technological goods. Can we imagine a CD player with a housing that is the result of the involvement of a craftsperson? How would this work? This might be a subject for discussion.

Craft and Cultural Meaning

Millie Creighton Neil Forrest Gerald Pocius

Millie R. Creighton

Nostalgia, Identity, and Gender:
Woven in 100 Per Cent Pure Silk

Millie R. Creighton is

Assistant Professor in the Department

of Anthropology and Sociology

at the University of British Columbia.

Paroles de nostalgie, d'indentité et de genre tissées de soie pure

Dissimulée dans une région obscure des Alpes japonaises, une petite entreprise familiale conserve son patrimoine du tissage de la soie en offrant des séminaires hebdomadaires avec hébergement pour les femmes urbaines en vacances. Cet article analyse la structure et le procédé des séminaires de tissage en révélant la manière par laquelle ils reflètent les pratiques de socialisation japonaises et les attitudes traditionalistes envers l'éducation. En scrutant les paradoxes créés lorsque le travail révolu du tissage de la soie en régions rurales s'est transformé en activités de loisirs pour les populations urbaines, cette communication illustre comment ces forfaits de voyage-artisanat concernent la réinvention de la tradition et l'affirmation renouvelée des valeurs rurales comme partie intégrante de la reconstruction moderne de l'identité japonaise. Les voix des femmes participant aux ateliers révèlent la renaissance de la participation des femmes aux activités artisanales en tant que métaphore de la résistance à l'hégémonie masculine, mise au point en plaçant sous contrôle féminin des activités longtemps réservées uniquement aux femmes.

Introduction

This paper explores the one-week residential silk-weaving seminars for women held in the Japanese Alps of Nagano Prefecture. These seminars exemplify processes that permeate Japanese society and culture, but they also have many parallels with the meanings of craft in contemporary Canadian society. Although there is a great deal of craft production in cities in Japan, these weaving seminars reflect a generalized romanticization of the country-side and a nostalgia for the pre-industrial past. Silk, and silk weaving, serve as dominant metaphors for the Japanese self, even though they are present in other parts of Asia. Crafts are similarly used in the construction of national identity elsewhere. For example, in both Canada and the United States quilting is a symbol of a national heritage, showing that a craft need not be unique to a particular society to be embraced as a cultural symbol. As in craft production elsewhere, gender issues are also woven into the production of silk in the Japanese seminars.

There are also parallels with economic differentiation in modern societies and with the often paradoxical nature of consumerism that surrounds craft. For William Morris, the commitment to craft meant a commitment to socialist thought so all people could participate in the beauty that can exist in everyday life. However, to make a living in the modern world, most craftspeople have to cater to affluent elites, and craft production has often been removed from the possible participation of the working-class groups once at its core.

The Weaving Workshop Retreats

The live-in weaving seminars are held in a remote part of the Japan Alps, once the heart of Japan's silk-weaving industry in the Meiji era (1868-1912). The local silk factories fostered Japan's industrialization and early economic development but exploited the labour of young rural women from poor families, who were often sold into silk-weaving contracts (Tsurumi 1990). Now, predominately urban, fairly affluent women travel here to spin and weave as a hobby. That some attempt was made to relate the learning experience to "traditionalism" is evident in the slogan of the workshop, *"Dento no naka de genzai o..."* This can be rendered as, "To construct the present based on tradition" or "Crafting our present from the heart of tradition."

The weaving workshops force us to question the dichotomy between work and leisure. This is a craft once learned as work and now learned in leisure as part of educating the self. The workshops reveal many similarities with the transmission of knowledge in the workplace, as presented in Rohlen's (1974) account of a bank and Kondo's (1990) more recent account of small businesses. Craft as self-education, or "working" at leisure on one's own self-development, serves a legitimating function. Travel in the guise of pilgrimage has long been used to legitimize sightseeing for the Japanese, something Graburn (1983) calls the "pray, pay, and play" philosophy of travel. The high cultural value placed on education in Japan legitimizes leisure pursuits that might otherwise seem self-indulgent. People can find *ikigai,* a reason for living, and a pathway to enlightenment through the earnest pursuit of a hobby (Creighton 1992, 50).

The week-long workshops, offered during four months of the year, are run by a Japanese couple who themselves exemplify the modern nostalgia for a lost past. The husband grew up in a weaving household but left it to follow the desirable elite track of salaried employee in a large firm. He later renounced this life, returning to his Nagano roots and the weaving background of his ancestors. His wife is a survivor of the atomic bombing of Hiroshima, a fact that plays into her own desires to lead a life that harmonizes with nature and affirms the value of handcrafted products. The sessions are always full, and many participants apply for several years before getting in. The participants are divided into two types – newcomers, and those who have participated before. This forms the basis of *senpai-kohai,* or senior-junior relationships. Those who have taken part before are *senpai* (seniors); newcomers are *kohai* (juniors).

New participants discover that their journey takes them precisely, and sometimes painfully, into the heart of the non-urban reality they have been romanticizing. One alights from the long-distance bus at a "station" consisting of a pole with a bus stop sign, a bench, and a telephone located in an otherwise totally remote mountainous area. After arriving at the workshops, newcomers find they are not fully integrated into activities. Returning participants are actively involved in their own pursuits, and Mr. *Sensei* (teacher)[1] is fully occupied with them, while Mrs. *Sensei* is busy with preparations for the week. Until the initial dinner meeting, newcomers are left on their own, with no assigned tasks. Interaction between them, all strangers at this point,

---

1 *Sensei* is a term of respect used for teachers and certain other professionals in Japan. Because both members of the couple who ran the workshops were also our teachers, it became the custom to differentiate them by using the referents *otoko sensei* (male teacher, or "Mr. Teacher") and *onna sensei* (female teacher, or "Mrs. Teacher").

is constrained, and after several walks around the natural environment, little is left to do. One is allowed to "relax," and this forced "relaxation" can become the most disliked "work" of the workshops. By the first dinner session, structure is less something imposed than something for which everyone longs. Likewise, the initial experience of being unattached and not integrated into group activities makes the incorporation into defined groups welcome.

Studies of Japanese schools, from nursery schools (Peak 1991; Lewis 1984; Tobin, Wu, and Davidson 1989; Hendry 1986) to high schools (Rohlen 1983) have dealt with the socialization of individuals into groups as part of the learning process. This also occurs in the weaving workshops. Although many activities are shared by all participants, creating a strong identification among all members of a session, the strongest bonds of group identity are formed in the A-*han* (A-group) and B-*han* (B-group), the two groups into which newcomers are divided. The approximately eight women in each of these groups spend nearly every moment of every day, from waking to sleeping, engaged together in the same activities at the same time.

The day begins at 5:00 or 5:30 a.m. Kondo describes how everyone on a spiritual retreat for company employees must awaken at 5:00 a.m., a practice that she relates to a cultural belief that waking early is the mark of an ethical person (Kondo 1990, 84). The weaving workshops make no stated assertion that the day begins as 5:00 a.m. Participants are told not to exert themselves too much, that they may take a nap (no one ever does), and that they need not wake up early. However, the dormitory windows have only rice paper sliding shutters, which block outside views but allow the sun to shine in. Since Japan does not have daylight saving time, this makes it a struggle not to awake at 5:00 a.m.

After breakfast the advanced students work independently while the A-group and B-group receive organized lessons. Then there is a mid-morning break for green tea and fruit. The fruit is always the local seasonal specialty, emphasizing connections with the natural environment of the place. This is followed by more group lessons, then lunch from 12:30 to 1:30 followed again by group lessons. At 3:00 p.m. every day, all workshop members participate in "radio exercises" that are broadcast daily throughout Japan. Since Japan has only one time zone, the radio exercises help synchronize the activities of many people throughout the country, creating a symbol of collective national identity in the process. Exercises are followed by the mid-afternoon break for green tea and fruit, again followed by group lessons. Dinner is at 7:00, followed by more individual tasks, such as weaving one's own sections of cloth or spinning thread. The daily schedule of seminar activities reflects an educational emphasis on "habituating the body." Participants habituate their bodies to anticipate the same activities at the same time every day, while training those bodies to perform the craft processes without thinking.

The workshops place a strong emphasis on a sense of process, rather than on achieving production; hence first-time participants spend little time actually weaving. For the first several days, new participants learn how to raise silk worms, how to boil the cocoons, how to remove the dead worms from the cocoons, how to make silk watting, how to spin thread, and how to dye threads with natural grasses they collect in the mountains. This reflects a belief that to have a full appreciation for the craft, one needs to understand the materials and all the preparatory work that precedes weaving. Preparing to craft means preparing the *kokoro* (heart-mind), as in calligraphy, where many people consider grinding the ink as essential to the spiritual process of learning as perfecting the style of written characters. As a participant, I can attest that one embraces a sense of awe and wonder at the nature of hand-woven goods when, through personal experience, one realizes what goes into every stage of the process from raising the worms and preparing the cocoons to spinning and dyeing before one can even begin to consider weaving.

Each group collectively chooses the lengthwise threads for its looms, sets their looms up together, and ties each of the three thousand lengthwise threads to three thousand corresponding threads that ended the previous piece. Each member of the group then weaves a section of each cloth, according to her own taste. Setting up the looms would be difficult for any one person new to this type of weaving. However, relying on each other, the members of the group are able to set up the looms without repeated coaching, and with no errors in tying the six thousand threads. This mutual assistance exemplifies themes that Yanagi (1989, 133-36) felt lie at the heart of craft. Yanagi believed that because craft allows individuals to rely on each other and on a tradition, nearly everyone has the capacity to create works of great beauty and that this does not necessitate individual creative genius.

A group of first-time
participants set up their looms together.
Credit: Millie Creighton

A group of women learn how to
remove silk worms from cocoons in
preparation for making silk batting.
Credit: Millie Creighton

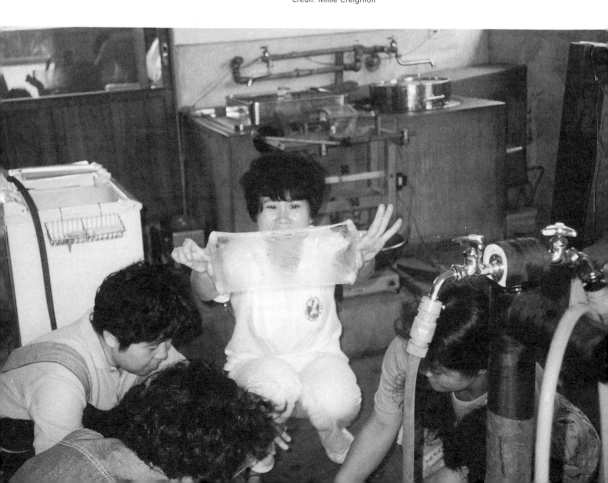

Three Metaphors: Nostalgia, Identity, Gender

According to Davis, nostalgia is part of a "collective search for identity" which "looks backward rather than forward, for the familiar rather than the novel, for certainty rather than discovery" (Davis 1979, 107, 108). The shift from an agrarian to an urban society, industrialization, westernization, and even Japan's modern affluence have all contributed to a sense of cultural loss and questions about cultural identity. The re-affirmation of traditional crafts such as silk weaving calms fears about a vanishing cultural identity and speaks to the nostalgia for a way of life from which people feel themselves increasingly separated.

Nostalgia has prompted great popular interest in crafts that are seen as traditional, and has led to a romanticization of the countryside – largely by and for urban dwellers. Moeran's (1984) study of a pottery community on the island of Kyushu shows how popular urban consumer fads affect the area, and the works of Ivy (1988) and Martinez (1990) reveal the influence of the nostalgia for a lost Japan on the domestic travel industry and on those Japanese who really do still live in rural or remote areas. The weaving seminars appear to be a rural, traditional phenomenon but are based in the reality of an urbanized, westernized, industrialized, and highly consumer-oriented modern Japan. The participants in the seminars, all women, are for the most part city dwellers who themselves travel to these representative parts of "lost Japan" during their holidays. Modern travel campaigns suggest that travelling to remote rural areas is a return to Japan's rural past and also to the Japanese *kokoro* (heart-mind), a *kokoro* that is non-rational, non-urban, and definitely non-Western (see Creighton, forthcoming). As Ivy (1988, 22) explains,

> the traveler's "self" equals an original Japanese self which equals the authentic *kokoro*, which in turn equals the rural, remote, non-American, and non-rational. Travel is the operator which connects the terms of the equation, by allowing the displacement of discovery to occur. Travel permits a temporary recuperation of a lost self.

The nostalgic mood within which much of the popular resurgence of crafts in Japan is embedded is thus associated with an ideal of life that harmonizes more fully with nature, where a sense of community is still strong, and where human life takes place within reciprocal obligations and support networks.

The weaving workshops are a modern attempt to construct cultural, collective, and personal identity. Silk becomes a symbol of the Japanese self, and silk weaving becomes a symbol of all Japanese tradition. By participating in the seminars one is not just learning to weave, or learning *a* craft, but learning a *Japanese* craft. Therefore, one is learning to be Japanese and what it means to be Japanese – the value of being Japanese – in the process.

The socialization and learning experiences within the workshops create a strong group identity. As in the larger society, these frameworks of group identity are multiple and overlapping, with one framework emerging as the strongest locus of identity. A strong sense of group identity develops among all participants during a session. However, group identity is strongest within smaller groups, in particular among the newcomers in the A-han and B-han who do everything together throughout the week and collectively make decisions about their looms and weaving materials.

Unlike many Western traditions, Japanese culture tends to de-emphasize individualism. The emphasis on group activity and merging the self with a group identity does not however, negate individuality. A metaphor for the relationship between personal and collective identity is given material manifestation in the woven products of seminar participants. All new participants weave four placemat-size pieces of cloth on four different looms. The lengthwise threads (warp) for the looms are either chosen by the group or already set in place by the instructors before the workshop begins. Each woman individually chooses her own crosswise threads (woof) for her segments. Thus each segment of cloth is both a collective product and an object affirming the individuality of each woman within the constraints of the group. Despite the fact that each cloth has exactly the same framework, or lengthwise threads running through it, there is amazing variation among the individually woven segments.

At the end of the week, just before the big *sayonara* party, the participants cut each cloth into segments so they can take their own pieces home. This is a highly ritualized and well photographed event, with all participants present. It is an extremely emotional climax, which brings many women near tears. After an intensive process of coming to understand everything that goes into making cloth, the women have great difficulty actually cutting it.

The woven silk cloth also becomes the material metaphor of personal relationships. For one week everyone is intensely joined together. Although addresses are exchanged, people generally realize that once they return to their normal lives, their ties to their fellow participants will recede. Separating, indeed *cutting,* the cloth, also stands for the separating of selves that the women realize is an implicit part of the final festive *sayonara* party. There is great sadness that the cloth is disturbed in any way, and the separation of the bonds which develop between participants is also recognized with great sadness.

Identity is strongly tied to constructions of gender, involving what it means to be male or female in any culture. Many Japanese women have eschewed the North American solution of careers as a means to self-identity and fulfilment, choosing instead to dedicate themselves to a craft or hobby pursuit (see Iwao 1993, Ueno 1988b). Often, these hobbies involve tasks once commonly part of women's domestic work, or tasks found in areas of employed work to which women were restricted. What is involved here is the transformation of traditional female work into hobbies or leisure activities.

There is a common assertion that, with industrialization, women's domestic work has been minimized through wonderful advances in labour-saving or time-saving appliances, and convenience goods. However, it often seems that what has been saved (or, more correctly, eliminated) of the traditionally defined domestic labour of women is precisely those types of work which were the most creative and fulfilling. Much of the mundane part of housework remains, while the things that provided the greatest satisfaction, such as cooking and baking (which can be referred to as "culinary crafts"), sewing, knitting, weaving, tatting, and so on, have been minimized or eliminated. This "hobbification" of what was formerly work also involves its gentrification status In order to return to these activities as hobbies, people must have the money and leisure to do so.

There is extensive discussion in Japan today about changes in female employment and career patterns. Much of this interest was heightened by the debates surrounding the passage of Japan's Equal Employment Opportunity Law in 1985, an act which was largely a response to international pressure.[2] While conducting research on Japan's new Equal Employment Opportunity Law in 1985 and 1986, I attempted to assess changes in women's commitment to work careers. Interviewing one established managerial woman, I asked whether she saw younger women orienting themselves more toward careers. She paused for a moment; then said she believed women were returning with greater interest and enthusiasm than ever before to handcrafts of all sorts, to work they could do with their hands. At first I saw no connection to the question I had asked, but when I con-

---

2 The year 1985 marked the close of the United Nations Decade of Women. An international charter calling for an end to discrimination against women was signed at the close of the period by member nations, and Japan was not going to be allowed to sign if it did not take measures toward eliminating discrimination against women by the end of 1985.

tinued getting responses such as these I realized my interviewees were making a connection between contemporary female consciousness and craft pursuits – a connection that linked contemporary female interest in crafts to issues of female gender identity under a system of hegemonic control.

From an outside perspective, Japan often appears noticeably lacking in a true "women's movement," because the women's movement in the West has largely been defined in terms of careers and work. According to the Japanese feminist Ueno (1988a), in the aftermath of the Equal Employment Opportunity Law, Japanese women are not embracing careers, but are instead saying "no" to this new form of exploitation that would require a double burden of work, in the domestic sphere and the public domain.

Ueno (1988b) believes modern Japanese women are trying to find personal development and fulfilment, not through a career, but in women's consumer activities. Initially this might be misinterpreted as the suggestion that superficial shopping experiences can bring a sense of deep satisfaction. However, since many avenues for education, learning, and self-development in contemporary Japan take place through consumer activities, Ueno's suggestion takes on a different meaning. For example, participants in the weaving seminars usually enrol through consumer-oriented cultural centres found in such places as department stores. Involvement in crafts is one response women are making, if not as a means of eliminating inequalities in status between the sexes, at least as a way of finding a less contested territory for self-discovery, development, and fulfilment. Japanese women's resurgent interest in handcrafts has characteristically involved embracing activities long defined as female pursuits. I would like to suggest that what appears to be women embracing a very traditionalistic model of gender definitions, can, in contrast, be understood as women returning to female domains of activity as a form of resistance against hegemonic processes.

There is a long-established distinction in anthropology between domestic and public spheres of activity (see Rosaldo 1974). In most cultures women are assigned the responsibility for organizing the domestic sphere, while men are more often defined in relationship to the public sphere. That status of women depends on how much access to the public realm they have, as well as the extent of separation between private and public spheres. This conceptual model can be enhanced when superimposed on the distinction between spheres of activity and spheres of control as discussed by Yanagisako (1985, 48-55).

Yanagisako differentiates between the "division of labour" and the "division of power" in the construction of male and female activities. This important distinction recognizes that being assigned to the activities of a particular sphere cannot be equated with having control over those activities. Clearly, Japanese women have long been assigned to the domestic sphere. However, in the traditional household, this was not the same as control over their own work in that sphere. As women return to crafts, they are indeed embracing activities that have long been defined as female, but they now control their participation in these activities and the products of their own labour. To help show this I offer a story presented by a participant of the first session I attended in 1986, along with the interpretation given to it by the women participating in 1992.

This woman's personal story mirrors the discourse of nostalgia involved in the transition from a rural pre-modern Japan to a highly urbanized, post-industrialized Japan. She was raised in a traditional rural extended family. Unlike most women of her age, she pursued an education that would lead to a profession, and at the time of her involvement in 1986 she was a thirty-year old pharmacist living and working in Tokyo. When she first heard of the seminars, this urban career woman recalled her rural childhood and how the sounds of her grandmother's silk loom reverberated throughout the large wooden farmhouse from dawn till dusk. She described this nostalgic memory as we were all looking at catalogues selling weaving equipment. Seeing the advertisements for high-priced looms she longed to buy but knew she could not afford, she sighed as she recalled a loom just like them that had stood in a room at home for years. "When my grandmother died," she said, "my mother burned it."

A Japanese proverb says that the father works, the son plays, and the grandson begs. Perhaps a modern version of this proverb, suggesting Japan's modern nostalgic identity crisis, could be restated as: the mother-in-law weaves in the Japanese tradition, the daughter-in-law throws away the loom to embrace westernization and modernization, and the granddaughter sulks over the loss of a culture. For this woman's grandmother, weaving was an essential part of a woman's household work. It meant clothing a family in the lean post-war years, or supplementing the family income. The value of the loom was lost on the mother. It was an anachronistic symbol of the past, as Japan was modernizing and becoming an industrialized nation. For the mother such domestic work was something from which to be liberated, the modern conveniences of life were welcomed. Now the granddaughter, only after the past is lost, recognizes the value in it and wishes to have back what her parents' generation threw away.

This story also reflects the nature of women's experience in Japan as defined by the agnatic kinship system. It can be interpreted as an act of resistance in a system that controls women by compelling them to control each other, represented most clearly in the tension-ridden relationship between mother-in-law and daughter-in-law. By burning the loom, the daughter-in-law symbolically destroys the yoke from which she has been freed by her mother-in-law's death.

In 1992 I told this story to women participating in the later workshops. Although many of them agreed with my ideas about the mother-in-law/daughter-in-law relationship, they interpreted the story as a metaphor of female resistance through the rejection of a process that controlled women rather than one in which women had any control. In the past, I was told by the participants, the women wove, but the men decided what to do with the cloth. Women would be prodded to work harder, to weave more and more, or better and better cloth. When the women finished weaving, the men would take the cloth to market to exchange for money in order to buy things that the men themselves wanted.

The women's comments show that a return to female craft activities does not mean embracing a state of subjugation. Women were embracing by choice, in their leisure time and at their own expense, precisely those activities they believed had once constrained women. Whereas before, these were domains of women's work under the control of men, now these were experienced by the women as domains of women's work which they themselves controlled.

Conclusion

The leisure hobby craft seminars described here illustrate the axiom that "making is metaphor." Weaving is a metaphor for social interaction, the woven cloth symbolizing ties woven between participants. Silk weaving is a metaphor of nostalgia for a lost Japanese past, and a marker of Japanese identity. It also represents a desire to return to involvement – physically and manually – in the creative and fulfilling processes of making handcraft objects, something people see as a loss resulting from modernization and mass production. Weaving becomes a metaphor of making that involves re-defining processes, long assigned to the female realm, as also under female control.

Although the instructors are well paid for the week-long hobby sessions, it would be wrong to imagine that they consider the financial rewards to be any more important than their proclaimed goals of maintaining Japan's traditional weaving crafts. Most of the women who attend the leisure hobby sessions will never come back; the few placemat-size cloths they take home will be all they ever weave. Although few participants out of the thousands who attend will go on to become professional or even committed weavers, their involvement as hobby enthusiasts – even if only for one week – is immensely important to the instructors. This can be seen through an analogy between craft and performance.

A performance requires an audience. Most of the Japanese performing arts, such as Noh, Kabuki, and Bunraku, require educated audiences that can comprehend, enjoy, and appreciate a good performance. Maintaining such traditions necessitates both training dedicated performers, and educating audiences to assure that there will be people capable of receiving the performance.

The weaving instructors have dedicated themselves to the performance of a craft and are fighting to make sure that as a representative "Japanese tradition" it does not fade from the modern scene. The perpetuation of the craft performance would mean little if the modern Japanese audience, or at least some members of it, were not trained to appreciate the craft performance. Thousands of women have passed through these weaving seminars and have recounted their experiences to female friends, relatives, or co-workers. Most of them will not become "weaving performers," but their deep experiential appreciation for all that is involved in the craft will remain. This helps ensure the continued existence of an understanding and appreciative audience for weaving in modern Japan. The presence of such a knowledgeable and appreciative audience cannot be separated from the goal of maintaining silk weaving as traditional craft performance.

References

Creighton, Millie R. 1992. "The Depaato: Merchandising the West while Selling Japaneseness." In *Re-Made in Japan: Everyday Life and Consumer Taste in a Changing Society,* ed. Joseph J. Tobin, pp. 42-57. New Haven: Yale University Press.

– – – forthcoming. "The Marketing of Tradition and Nostalgia in the Japanese Travel Industry." In *Travel Discourse and the Pacific Rim,* ed. Eva-Marie Kroller. Vancouver: University of British Columbia Press.

Davis, Fred. 1979. *Yearning for Yesterday: A Sociology of Nostalgia.* New York: Free Press.

Graburn, N.H.H. 1983. *To Pray, Pay and Play: The Cultural Structure of Japanese Domestic Tourism.* Series B no. 26. Aix-en-Provence: Centre des hautes Études touristiques.

Hendry, Joy. 1986. *Becoming Japanese: The World of the Pre-School Child.* Manchester: Manchester University Press.

Ivy, Marilyn. 1988. "Tradition and Difference in the Japanese Mass Media." *Public Culture* 1, no. 1: 21-29.

Iwao Sumiko. 1993. *The Japanese Woman: Traditional Image and Changing Reality.* New York: The Free Press.

Kondo, Dorinne K. 1990. *Crafting Selves: Power, Gender, and Discourses of Identity in a Japanese Workplace.* Chicago: University of Chicago Press.

Lewis, Catherine C. 1984. "Cooperation and Control in Japanese Nursery Schools." *Comparative Education Review* 28, no. 1: 69-84.

Martinez, D. P. 1990. "Tourism and the Ama: The Search for a Real Japan." In *Unwrapping Japan: Society and Culture in Anthropological Perspective,* ed. Eyal Ben-Ari, Brian Moeran, and James Valentine, 97-116. Honolulu: University of Hawaii Press.

Moeran, Brian. 1984. *Lost Innocence: Folk Craft Potters of Onta, Japan.* Berkeley: University of California Press.

Peak, Lois. 1991. *Learning to Go to School in Japan: The Transition from Home to Preschool Life.* Berkeley: University of California Press.

Rohlen, Thomas P. 1974. *For Harmony and Strength: Japanese White-Collar Organization in Anthropological Perspective.* Berkeley: University of California Press.

– – – 1983. *Japan's High Schools.* Berkeley: University of California Press.

Rosaldo, Michelle Zimbalist. 1974. "Woman, Culture and Society: A Theoretical Overview." In *Woman, Culture and Society,* ed. Michelle Zimbalist Rosaldo and Louise Lamphere, 17-42. Stanford: Stanford University Press.

Tobin, Joseph, David Wu, and Dana Davidson. 1989. *Preschool in Three Cultures: Japan, China and the United States.* New Haven: Yale University Press.

Tsurumi, E. Patricia. 1990. *Factory Girls: Women in the Thread Mills of Meiji Japan.* Princeton, N.J.: Princeton University Press.

Ueno Chizuko. 1988a. "The Japanese Women's Movement: The Counter-Values to Industrialism." In *The Japanese Trajectory: Modernization and Beyond,* ed. Gavin McCormack and Sugimoto Yoshio 167-185. Cambridge: Cambridge University Press.

– – – 1988b. *"Onnaen" ga yo no naka o Kaeru* [Women's Networking Changing the Society]. Tokyo: Nihonkeizai Shinbunsha.

Yanagi Soetsu. 1989. *The Unknown Craftsman: A Japanese Insight into Beauty.* Tokyo: Kodansha.

Yanagisako, Sylvia Junko. 1985. *Transforming the Past: Tradition and Kinship Among Japanese Americans.* Stanford: Stanford University Press.

Neil Forrest

Reclaiming the Role
of Craft in Architecture

Neil Forrest is a ceramist and

Assistant Professor at the Nova Scotia

College of Art and Design.

Une métaphore sans domicile

L'artisanat pourrait à première vue être décrit comme le mariage de la technologie et de la production manuelle. La technologie sert à décrire l'utilisation logique des matériaux naturels convenables dans le but de répondre à des besoins concrets spécifiques à l'intérieur d'une culture ou d'une civilisation. La production et la technologie (le travail et ses moyens) amènent une conséquence intéressante, celle de l'utile qui appelle la beauté. Des objets utiles ont traditionnellement fourni l'occasion d'exprimer l'ingéniosité esthétique du créateur. Cette ingéniosité esthétique se transforme en un langage visuel de consensus pour une culture telle qu'exprimée dans la poterie fonctionnelle, les textiles, les meubles et les bijoux. L'artisanat de ce siècle doit être revu en fonction de la production.

L'artisanat constitue un des systèmes symboliques de notre culture. L'artisanat tend à être documenté et reconnu à travers ses objets rituels et de prestige et constitue donc une forme d'art qui a été, jusqu'à tout récemment, interprétée par les anthropologues plutôt que par les historiens de l'art. Toutefois, les objets de prestige de notre culture ont passé de l'artisanat à l'art sous la pression successive des forces de la Renaissance et de l'industrialisation. L'église et l'aristocratie, mécènes des objets d'artisanat de prestige en Occident, ont été remplacées par le musée et la classe moyenne. Maintenant, nous n'avons qu'une seule église par ville!

Les artisans modernes ont démontré qu'ils pouvaient bel et bien identifier des stratégies pour perfectionner l'aspect significatif de leur oeuvre et ils ont reconnu la nécessité
de maintenir leur pertinence. La question que nous devons nous poser n'est pas de
savoir si les artisans peuvent adopter les stratégies actuelles des autres arts visuels et littéraires, mais si notre domaine peut et doit demeurer artisanal étant donné les conditions traditionnelles qui régissent l'artisanat. Celles-ci comprendraient : utilisation/valeur
moyen de production nature égalitaire contextuel/au corps, à l'architecture L'utilisation
unique de l'artisanat est une préoccupation importante. Le début de cet exposé sera consacré à la dislocation de la signification dans le domaine des métiers d'art et on proposera
la nécessité de définir et d'utiliser l'artisanat en raison de sa capacité et de son mandat
de servir son contexte. L'artisanat a toujours été la plus contextuelle des formes d'art.

Nous aborderons l'affinité caractéristique de l'artisanat avec l'environnement construit – son rôle en architecture. Je soutiens que l'artisanat peut répondre à des besoins
particuliers et généraux dans notre environnement habité qui présentera toujours un
nombre infini de défis intellectuels, physiques et formels. Cette communication vise à
fournir des exemples historiques de la relation entre l'artisanat et l'architecture. La formation des artisans, des architectes et des concepteurs sera analysée en vue de découvrir comment les domaines d'enseignement ont influencé les relations entre ces arts jadis
coopératifs.

As a ceramics rookie in the early 1970s, I assumed my field had youth, membership, and unlimited potential. The notion of the unencumbered youth of
ceramics was in reality a lack of historical knowledge on my part. In postwar North America, energetic heros and teaching academies had resuscitated studio craft. However, as we try to measure the stature of ceramics and
its kin, it is evident that crafts are being neglected by patrons and arts institutions.

Craft professionals have increasingly devoted much attention to redefining the boundaries of craft in order to share in the recognition and status
accorded the fine arts. Nevertheless, there is an identity crisis within our
own ranks. While we sort through our questions, craft's recent brush with
success is fading and installation and inter-media arts are poaching on craft
territory. Are craftspeople hoping not to be confused with the fine arts or
be considered their handmaiden? At this crossroads, craft must reassert its
uniqueness, undertake new ventures, and rethink its pedagogy to survive
and flourish. These goals can and should be pursued within the traditional
mandate of craft. Since the contemporary "craft community has had to

create its own infrastructures," such as guilds and public craft museums, craft practitioners, not the arts bureaucrats and university administrators, must again be the agents of change (Inglis 1987). One way to accomplish this is to reclaim our historic presence within architecture.

Our popular conception of craft suggests we cherish handmade objects more for sentiment than for practicality and invention. We think of craft as a discrete body of objects like jewellery, weavings, and pottery, but the past informs us that crafts provided for all utilitarian, ritual, and status requirements. It is reasonable to assert that for early civilizations craft *was* technology (Wulff 1966). Improvements in agricultural implements or military weaponry would have been synonymous with the progress of craft.

From time immemorial, craft producers have been respected as clever and capable. In 1 Kings, chapter 7, we are told that King Solomon recruited a bronze worker named Huram, known for his intelligence and experience as a craftsman. His task was no less than to create all the ritual and architectural fixtures for the Temple of the Ark of the Covenant and Solomon's palace. Craft has a remarkable history that combines science, technology, dexterity, and artistic invention. Ruskin and Morris held the view that craft is inclusive, that it "embraces the high and low, the fine arts and the vernacular" (Craig 1981). This idea continues to have merit, although my remarks concentrate on the conscious and explicit aspect of craft.

The architectural historian Spiro Kostoff made a wonderful connection when he said, "Buildings are artifacts." This remark allows us to imagine the historical relationship of crafted objects to buildings. Both fields represent the accumulated skill and insight of a group or individual. Kostoff cites New England barns for their "honesty of materials and execution" and American architect Louis Kahn's "concrete walls of Doric purity" (Kostoff 1988, June/July). If we begin to speculate on the origins of architecture and craft, we might need to visualize the site of a holy tree or holy stone. These magical places had to be marked, consecrated, and revered. For this a ritual practice was created, thereby shaping the space around the ritual. Eventually, as crafted objects replaced the natural, the sites became shrines; hence the confluence of craft and architecture (Armstrong 1981).

As the study of architecture is formalized, it examines structures and their system of signs in relation to evolving social and cultural conditions. Built structures are a means of articulating ideas and organizing activity for individuals, families, and society. It is these structures that accompany and shape the patterns of use within. The patterns of ritual use are revealed clearly in places of religious worship. If we consider the Christian Church, we see that the building program continuously reflects and adjusts the church's forms of worship. When Christianity was legitimized, its adherents began to use architecture and craft to give ritual expression to the mass and baptism. The depiction of biblical stories in mosaics profoundly stirred the congregation and altered devotional practices. In the centuries following Christ, the purpose of the church building was thoroughly ritualistic: to venerate a specific object such as a tomb, rock, bone, or baptismal font.

So-called occasional buildings were erected to house these objects. These buildings could be as simple as a canopy raised above the object or could be permanently dedicated like a stone baptistery with its "dome of heaven." I remember my surprise when first encountering a relic, the finger bones of a Christian saint perched in a strange and glorious toy house: the craft equivalent of the occasional building (Kostoff 1985).

As mystic and religious ritual practices connected architecture and craft in the past, so today do our social and familial rituals. Functional craft objects such as tableware, clothing, jewellery, carpets, perfume bottles, and the like, are geared not only to human physical requirements, but to the social and personal landscape. A dinner gathering uses certain utensils to create an appropriate atmosphere. Will it be the dignified porcelain or the bright earthenware pottery when the in-laws come for dinner? If this is their inaugural dinner, it's surely a rite of passage for the hosts. The dishes will help either to elevate or to ease the decorum. If the hosts opt for classic porcelain, its elegance implies that the event is a formal occasion. The effect on human behaviour and the power of signification are part of craft.

The exchange flows the other way too, because the craft object is informed by the participants and by the event itself. The participants come and assign meaning to the event and its attending objects. Domestic craft objects are chosen to fit comfortably into the democratic and less hierarchical setting of our home – and are therefore mistaken or mundane objects, unlike tomb relics, chalices, and stained glass, which bespeak religious and institutional values. In a museum visit to the tomb accessories of Tutankhamen, anyone can grasp the importance of expertly crafted objects in the rites of worship and death. Symbolic objects were so valuable to the ancients that they took their crafts to the grave.

In Western religion as well, authority and worship are intrinsically tied to the visual component of art, craft, and architecture. The humanist measurement of classical architecture was discarded by the church in favour of the sublime. The Gothic program made it clear to Christians that the church was a surrogate for Christ's teachings and had to be glorious. Not only was the grammar of portals and rosette windows an expression of doctrine, but so too was the disposition of portable censers, mosaics, and reliquaries. Both the portable object and the integrated ornament determine the cycle of worship. The propagandist function of craft was crucial because architectural decoration had to extol the triumphs of the liturgy, the agonies of the Passion and the apocalyptic Second Coming (Kostoff 1985, chap. 21, passim).

Our history of ecclesiastical architecture in the West demonstrates a multitude of ritual and symbolic uses for craft, quite apart from the domestic and technological. But the arrival of the Enlightenment, with its democracy, social justice, and nationalism, curtailed patronage from the church. With the great religious program bankrupt, the modern era was less dependent on the services of architectural craft. By contrast, the fine arts flourished in this environment. Scholars developed the strategy of collecting and studying the products of the Renaissance ideal. The modern artist, an independent thinker and brilliant innovator, was rewarded with the art museum. The down side was that crafts became less important in providing the propaganda and the pizzazz for buildings. This was soon to be delivered by the architect himself, who was also a prodigy of the Renaissance hothouse.

One additional development banished craft from architecture: the age of industry. Painting and sculpture easily resisted technology, but crafts could accept the division of labour and machine production of industry. Painting and sculpture were valuable only if original; generally, craft could endure duplication without losing its worth – it retains its use and value. While folk crafts were marginalized by the factory and its industrial designer, the industrialization of building components became a tonic for architecture. As a vocation, architecture was not threatened by the factory for two reasons: during the Renaissance, architects had evolved from master builders to designers, and they were needed to produce fresh plans for every client.

I have emphasized the portable type of craft within the spaces of architecture. As we investigate ornament as an integral part of construction, it's clear that architecture has continuously used craft within its fabric – stone carving and woodwork for example. One can visit any period of Western architecture from classical to modern and interpret architectural mythology through its integrated ornament. The German baroque and softer rococo present such an example of conceptual and material interdependence.

Church façade of glazed
ceramic tiles in Valega, Portugal.
Credit: Neil Forrest

Decorated ceiling in the
Music Room of the Ali Qapu
Palace, Isfahan, Iran.
Late fourteenth century.
Credit: Neil Forrest

Decorated ceiling in the
Music Room of the Ali Qapu
Palace, Isfahan, Iran.
Late fourteenth century.
Credit: Neil Forrest

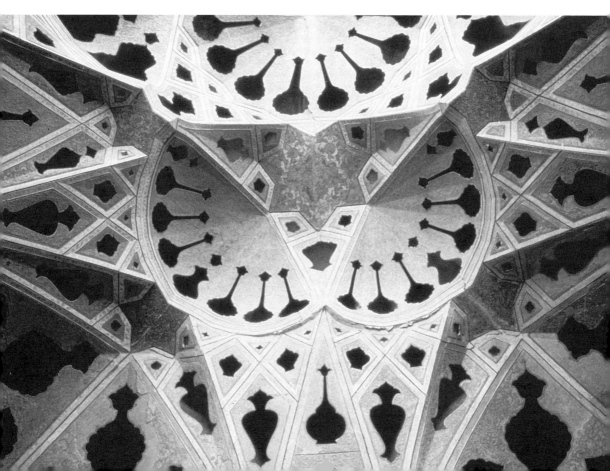

Baroque was theatre, an acid trip of materials and images, what the Germans called *Gesamtkunstwerk* — "a total work of art." Inside the buildings, emotion was generated by the fusion of painting, ornament, and sculpture. This impressionistic concoction was aimed at creating great illusions that denied structural anatomy. The extravagant painting schemes and flowing ornament camouflaged columns and arches. Not surprisingly, the designers of the German baroque were masons, stuccoists, and painters of craft origins (Norberg-Shulz 1972, chap. 5).

If the architecture of the church and palace provide countless examples of craft ornament, the search might seem to narrow with the dawning of Modernity and its profusion of styles. Eccentric styles like the modernismo of Spain spring to mind as rich in craft, adapting the romantic regional vernacular or novel style to advanced steel frame construction. Antonio Gaudi attempted to renew the handcrafted character of Barcelona architecture with Catalonian brick, tile, wrought iron, and woodwork, moulded into a metaphorical and sculptural architecture. Yet Gaudi was not a solitary voice of ornamental modernism early in this century: there was Horta in Belgium, and Guimard and Perret in France. Wagner and Olbrich were notable in Austria. In Scotland there was Mackintosh. Webb, Voysey, and Ashbee were in the English Arts and Crafts; the United States had Sullivan and Wright.

Compelling as it is to glorify craft achievements within such flamboyant styles as the German baroque and Catalonian modernismo, most ornamental architecture passes unnoticed in official histories, which favour the monumental and avant-garde. If we examine Portuguese tiled buildings, however, we uncover a delightful synthesis of craft in architecture. Without designers of international reputation, Portugal nurtured an ambitious tile industry to achieve an aesthetic and economical signature for its buildings from the sixteenth to the twentieth century.

We should not forget that North American designers used ornament without interruption into the mid-twentieth century. American academic architecture refined earlier styles: beaux-arts, colonial revival, mission, art deco, etc. Of the camps in academic architecture in the early twentieth century, the beaux-arts and "organic" schools welcomed ornament, either by following historical models or by allowing materials to dictate (Gowans 1992, 216). By contrast, the modernists who preached against ornament were the much smaller voice in American architecture. But by mid-century, the international style became the dominant approach of modernism, emphasizing planes and using synthetic and light-weight materials. This chapter of architecture removed conventional signifiers, such as the explicit definition of each floor on the building's façade. Cocky and dogmatic, modernism claimed to be scientific, non-hierarchical, and universal. Yet its fate was to be identified with the corporate and government elite.

Architecture is now seeking to experience itself beyond the effortless manipulation of pure spaces and planes. The technological advances of steel frame, concrete, and curtain wall construction have been formally played out during the international style, and architecture is again searching for its identity, using semantic instruments like ornament and decoration. The utility of ornament in classical architecture was manifold, but its principal function was to emphasize structure or symbolize it. Given that ornament is once again welcome, craft must assert its presence differently in buildings whose structures are light-weight and invisible. Although craft may not determine the sculptural space of architecture, it can explore the programmatic meaning, using its own vast repertoire of iconography, which allows for intimate and personal references. Architectural craft, dormant during late modernism, has an opportunity to discover its potential within post-modern architecture and pursue humanistic ventures in this non-doctrinaire climate.

Craft can be an engine of contemporary architecture by thinking of itself as an organizing method. This was the case in pre-modern periods. The design of early churches, for example, was instructed by the reliquaries that required niches within the nave. Another organizing method is the unit of craft itself, the tile, brick, plank, or even a unit of weaving used as a design tool. A third organizing strategy is to develop the texture and iconography of architectural spaces as an alternative to modernism's preoccupation with spatial gymnastics.

When a building or utilitarian craft object is made, an assumption should follow: these forms become a host for additional information. To that end, both disciplines operate on two levels: craft objects provide a service (a cup delivers tea) and elevate that experience (it is glazed with a motif). Similarly, a building provides spaces to serve human activity and elevates the experience of use (Kuspit 1987). Traditionally, craft ornament was essential to enhance the experience of use. The modernist concept of engineering universal spaces displaced traditional ornament. Regardless of the sensibility possessed by masters like Mies Van der Rohe and Le Corbusier, their legacy is, unfortunately, a formulaic approach to design that is devoid of material beauty. In contemporary architecture, the absence of variety in the texture of materials is an opportunity for the craft disciplines. The haptic and intimate scale of traditional craft media is one way to increase the sensory participation of the building's user. Craft input is many layers of new information and animation. It can be the sensation and theatre that contest the poverty of modern reductivism. Craft offers a semantic perspective rather than an architectural technique.

The American architect Robert Venturi, in his seminal work, *Learning from Las Vegas,* argues for the notion of the "decorated shed": that structure and space are at the service of the program, and ornament is applied independently of them. In other words: applied decoration. Applied decoration, of course, isn't a new idea, just new to our generation. In fact, it follows Alberti's dictum that beauty comes from the harmony of proportions and ornament is added. Venturi contends the notion of "the decorated" is more appropriate for our time than the heroic stance of modernist architecture (Venturi et al. 1982). His point is refreshing: that we seek to experience the richness of architecture in the ordinary. Venturi's strategy is thus to take ordinary architecture and invest it with symbolism. Decoration is his vehicle, rendered in simple graphic vocabulary available from the factory. What Venturi doesn't invoke is the emotive and haptic properties of decorative materials.

Alberti drew the distinguishing line between the architect and architectural craftsman in the fifteenth century, when he declared, "The carpenter [in other words, the craftsman] is but an instrument in the hands of the architect" (Jackson 1993). I recommend that we rethink Alberti's bias, especially now that the education of craftspeople and architects is of similar sophistication. Here I am setting aside the more populist idea of craft learned by life and custom, and referring to professional craftspeople conversant with design methodology. The professional who becomes an architectural craftsperson will be of a new breed, able to design from a craft-based knowledge.

Architectural craft will be an urban practice, undertaken alongside other design professionals and in design and production teams. Architectural craftspeople must be versatile and adept at combining construction and craft materials and capable of executing the designs of others as well as their own.

The architectural team should involve craftspeople right from the conception of the design, in order to study issues of program and context. If architectural craft is to be meaningful, it cannot wait outside until the building is fully designed. The after-the-fact invitation to the craftsperson perpetuates the clichés of hangings and murals. Craft needs to respond to the design concept and serve the building. Recall the idea of craft as an organizing unit in society, able to stimulate and communicate design issues. We must express ideas that are unique to craft, distinct from painting and sculpture.

I cannot tell you what craft in architecture will look like, but we can find answers by asking our students. They might work on pavilions, gardens, parks, and fixtures in addition to conventional settings. Since craft education has found its place in the academy alongside art and architecture, we are able to appreciate each other's language and exchange ideas as equals. In our visual art and architecture schools, imaginative introductory and special project courses can be taught collaboratively at key points in a student's education. Craft students can become familiar with architectural theory by studying the language, signs, and symbols of buildings. Introductory architecture courses would address issues of site, program, and design. At the other campus, the art school provides an equivalent introduction to craft and visual art issues for architecture students. Project courses, the second phase, gives students a chance to collaborate. Working in teams, craft and architecture students can find strategies that bring each other's issues and skills into play.

Craft and architecture need their own mythologies and identity. We should encourage the opportunity for some to move their own discipline closer to the margins of the other.

Joint ventures with architecture will offer a vehicle for craft expression, and develop a new audience for craft.

Bibliography

Armstrong, Robert. 1981. *Powers of Presence: Consciousness, Myth and Affecting Presence.*
    Philadelphia: University of Pennsylvania Press.
Bouillon, Jean-Paul. 1989. *Art Deco 1903-1940.* New York: Rizzoli.
Brolin, Brent. C. 1980. *Architecture in Context.* New York: Van Nostrand Reinhold.
Cohen, Judith. 1988. *Cowtown Moderne.* College Station: Texas A & M Press.
Craig, Robert. 1981. "Ruskin, Morris and Maybeck," in *Language in Architecture.* Washington,
    D.C.: Association of Collegiate Schools of Architecture.
Ellis, Charlotte. 1986. "Public Housing as Realization of an Artist's Fantasy." *Architecture,* Sept.
Gowans, Alan. 1992. *Styles and Types of North American Architecture.* Icon Editions. New York:
    Harper Collins.
Hillier, Bevis. 1968. *Pottery and Porcelain, 1700-1914.* New York: Meredith.
Inglis, Steven. 1987. "The Island of Craft... and an Outgoing Tide." *Ontario Crafts,* Fall.
Jackson, Tony. 1993. Interview. Halifax, Aug.

Janson, H.W. 1983. *History of Art*. New York: Prentice-Hall.

Jencks, Charles A. 1977. *The Language of Post Modern Architecture*. New York: Rizzoli.

Julius, John, ed. 1979. *Great Architecture of the World*. New York: Bonanza.

Kostoff, Spiro. 1985. *A History of Architecture*. New York: Oxford.

– – – 1988. "Comment." *American Craft,* June/July.

Krier, Rob. 1982. *Rob Krier on Architecture*. New York: St. Martin's.

Kuspit, Donald. 1987. "Ceramic Considerations," closing address, National Council for Education in the Ceramic Arts (NCECA). *New Art Examiner* 15: supplement BD-O.

Mackay, David. 1989. *Modern Architecture in Barcelona*. New York: Rizzoli.

Mead, Christopher. 1991. *Houses by Bart Prince*. Albuquerque, New Mexico: University of New Mexico Press.

Meco, Jose. 1988. *The Art of the Azulejo in Portugal*. N.p.: Bertrand.

Norberg-Shulz, Christian. 1972. *Baroque Architecture*. New York: H.N. Abrams.

Ruskin, John. [1880] 1989. *The Seven Lamps of Architecture*. New York: Dover.

de Sola-Morales, Ignasi. 1990. *Jujol*. Barcelona: Poligrafa.

Speidel, Manfred, ed. 1991. *Team Zoo*. New York: Rizzoli.

Troy, Nancy. 1991. *Modernism and the Decorative Arts in France*. New Haven, Conn.: Yale University Press.

Venturi, Robert, Denise Scott Brown, and Steven Izenour. 1982. *Learning from Las Vegas,* Part 2. Cambridge, Mass.: M.I.T. Press.

Wines, James. 1987. *De-Architecture*. New York: Rizzoli International.

Wulff, Hans. 1966. *The Traditional Crafts of Persia*. Cambridge, Mass.: M.I.T. Press.

Gerald L. Pocius – Respondent

Craft and Cultural Meaning

Gerald L. Pocius is Professor of Folklore

and Co-Director of the Centre for Material

Culture Studies at Memorial

University of Newfoundland in St. John's.

Résumé

Dans chaque culture, les produits de tout métier d'art véhiculent un certain nombre de significations. Toute forme créée de main humaine peut toucher à plusieurs dimensions dont celles de nostalgie, de rapports de pouvoir (y compris entre les sexes) et d'identité. Pour ce qui est de la nostalgie, les objets artisanaux sont souvent liés à l'idée d'un passé idyllique, que ce dernier soit réel ou imaginaire. Un tel lien peut éveiller la nostalgie d'un mode de vie révolu, fréquemment réinterprété selon les valeurs contemporaines. Dans certains cas, en fait, la nostalgie s'invente un passé qui n'a jamais existé, un passé dominé par certains genres d'objets artisanaux. Il arrive aussi que la nostalgie accentue l'aspect manuel de la production, tout en minimisant d'autres éléments plus importants comme les sources de conception ou les matériaux. Le métier peut toucher aux rapports de pouvoir, entre individus ou entre groupes. En ce qui concerne plus spécifiquement les sexes, bon nombre des activités désignées comme des métiers ont traditionnellement relevé du domaine masculin, tandis que les choses moins concrètes ou moins durables réalisées par les femmes ne sont pas reconnues dans cette catégorie. Ces rapports de pouvoir sont aussi entretenus par les arbitres du bon goût, ceux qui décident de ce qui est acceptable en tant qu'objet artisanal esthétiquement valable, et ce qui ne l'est pas. Il est possible qu'un objet étiqueté comme kitsch par les professionnels des métiers d'art soit l'objet fabriqué à la main le plus important aux yeux d'autres groupes. Le métier peut aussi devenir un véhicule associé à la classe sociale dans la mesure où divers types d'objets, créés par nécessité dans un groupe, deviennent des réalisations de loisirs dans un autre groupe.

Enfin, les métiers d'art deviennent un moyen de stimuler l'identité, tant individuelle que collective. Les nations se créent souvent une identité en associant certains métiers d'art avec ce qu'elles considèrent l'essence de leur génie national. Dans d'autres cas, elles favorisent une esthétique nationale qui produit des objets qui suivent des règles de conception largement acceptées. Dans le cas des artisanats traditionnels d'Europe, mais aussi dans celui des artisanats de sociétés non européennes plus restreintes, l'identité du groupe a été renforcée par la création de certaines formes partagées par l'ensemble du groupe parce que le partage d'un langage artistique commun a encouragé la création d'un éventail d'objets auxquels chaque membre du groupe pouvait s'identifier. Toutefois, dans le contexte occidental moderne, l'identité est souvent créée par une esthétique de l'individualité, de la différence. En fait, face à la généralisation de cette recherche de l'originalité dans les métiers d'art, les sociétés modernes cherchent de nouveaux objets communs (qui sont souvent produits en série), pour créer des différences d'identité reconnaissables dans le monde de l'objet ouvré. Pourtant, en fin de compte, les recherches ethnographiques portant sur les sociétés passées et présentes indiquent que la valeur d'activités concrètes comme l'artisanat vient souvent après celle d'autres créations moins tangibles.

We can look at craft in two ways.[1] We can say that somehow the object which is fashioned has an inherent quality that exists apart from its initial context – a timeless creation, an affecting presence (to use Robert Plant Armstrong's term) through which all peoples can react directly to that object.[2] Or we can argue that craft is an arbitrary concept, culture-bound, and defined by every culture and every period in different ways. We can think of craft worlds (borrowing from Howard Becker's *Art Worlds*) – a series of objects, creators, exhibitors, and taste makers – as social constructs that

1 I would like to thank Shane O'Dea, who commented on an earlier version of this essay.

2 Robert Plant Armstrong's most accessible work in which he examines this concept is The Affecting Presence: An Essay in Humanistic Anthropology (Urbana: University of Illinois Press, 1971); see also his Wellspring: On the Myth and Source of Culture (Berkeley: University of California Press, 1975); and The Powers of Presence: Consciousness, Myth and the Affecting Presence (University of Pennsylvania Press, 1981). For an analytical model that attempts to explore ways implied by Armstrong see Jules Prown, "On the 'Art' in Artifacts," in Gerald L. Pocius, ed., Living in a Material World: Canadian and American Approaches to Material Culture, Social and Economic Papers 19 (St. John's: Institute of Social and Economic Research, Memorial University, 1991), 144-55.

are created in reaction to a society's needs and beliefs at different times.[3] Often, research on crafts parallels the two ends of this dichotomy: whether an object is studied strictly on its own for its aesthetic dimensions or used as a means to study social values and beliefs.[4]

The essays by Neil Forrest and Millie Creighton deal with materials that I feel address a number of crucial issues of craft worlds, of how we fashion our artifacts, not in any logical way, but in an attempt somehow to create meaning in our own particular social context. I will use the three concepts that Creighton employs in her paper as a point of departure. First, the idea of nostalgia.[5]

It seems that craft often becomes associated with some past era, and therefore many crafts become vehicles for nostalgia. This is curious, given that so many other objects (such as the rectangular house) or practices (such as our eating patterns) can often claim equally long lineages. But why is the practice of craft judged today by how it does or does not resemble earlier patterns? Why are crafts valued more if they are considered traditional and have a long historical lineage? All things we make today are in one sense modern, but a culture will then associate a nostalgic past with some of these. We are thus inventing our past – our traditions – through objects that express our own modern values (the handmade, non-mechanized, natural).[6] Is this accurate?

We romanticize earlier epochs – the medieval world of Morris and Ruskin, for example – as a time when what we consider as craft was an integral part of daily life.[7] Small groups of artists created works for local use, drawing on individual talent as well as accepted aesthetics. Yet success, perhaps, came from this common body of shared aesthetics. The individual

3 Howard Becker, Art Worlds (Berkeley: University of California Press, 1982); see also John Michael Vlach and Simon H. Bronner, "Introduction," in their Folk Art and Art Worlds. American Folklife and Material Culture (Ann Arbor: UMI Press, 1986), 1-10.

4 These two approaches are critiqued in Sally Price, Primitive Art in Civilized Places (Chicago: University of Chicago Press, 1989). An early statement is Robert Redfield, "Art and Icon," reprinted in Charlotte M. Otten, ed., Anthropology and Art: Readings in Cross-Cultural Aesthetics, American Museum Sourcebooks in Anthropology (Garden City: Natural History Press, 1971), 39-65.

5 Interestingly enough, the notion of nostalgia has its origins in the idea of homesickness and therefore relates to concerns about identity discussed below. See Jean Starobinski, "The Idea of Nostalgia," Diogenes 54 (1966): 81-103.

6 Much has been recently written on the idea of the "invention of tradition"; the original statement in is Eric Hobsbawn, "Introduction: Inventing Traditions," in Eric Hobsbawn and Terence Ranger, eds., The Invention of Tradition (Cambridge: Cambridge University Press, 1983) 1-14.

7 The medievalist romantic argument of Ruskin and Morris is eloquently summarized in Henry Glassie, All Silver and No Brass: An Irish Christmas Mumming (Bloomington: Indiana University Press, 1975), 53-67.

often bowed to the will of the group in questions of design and kept his idiosyncrasies well under control. Our modern ideal of creativity – of uniqueness – was not the ideal of traditional designers, who valued, rather, common designs and forms.[8]

Our interest in this pre-mechanized world, in short, emphasizes production – the way objects were made – and de-emphasizes the aesthetic constraints and the demands of the consumer of the time.[9] Nostalgia sees the hand working, not the mind limited by what was locally acceptable or by who could afford it. We blind ourselves to the presence of the market and limited design options when we emphasize many hands engaged in craft. What was the real nature of craft in these earlier, often romanticized times?[10]

Next comes the question of gender, which is really subsumed under the larger question of power or hegemony. Millie Creighton deals with female crafts, Neil Forrest in his medieval world with what are essentially male crafts. Forrest deals with craft as a modern occupation, whereas Creighton is concerned with how craft becomes a leisure activity. This juxtaposing of male and female, labour and leisure, leads me to a more fundamental question. How much of what we now label as crafts were primarily things that were made by males? We see the medieval cathedral with glass and metal, wood, stone, and paint, all the products of males. There were specifically female crafts (often textiles), as in Japan. But in many places, most female crafts often were ephemeral and left no visible mark on our craft lineage. Women made bread, painted the landscape with flowers, created the sculptures of room arrangements in their homes.[11] But the very definition of craft we often work with leaves us dangerously tolerant of the biased power arrangements of our highly gendered past. Where are these *other* crafts in our galleries and catalogues? Or craft conferences?

8 The typical assumption that traditional crafts are influenced by community aesthetics at the expense of individual creativity is discussed in John Michael Vlach, "'Properly Speaking': The Need for Plain Talk About Folk Art," in Vlach and Bronner, eds., Folk Art and Art Worlds, 13-26. A different view from Vlach can be found in Gerald L. Pocius, "Gossip, Rhetoric and Objects: A Sociolinguistic Approach to Newfoundland Furniture," in Gerald W. R. Ward, ed., Perspectives on American Furniture (New York: Norton, for Winterthur Museum, 1989), 57-85. For a range of essays debating this issue see Daniel P. Biebuyck, ed., Tradition and Creativity in Tribal Art (Berkeley: University of California Press, 1969).

9 Scholars are now realizing that the effects of consumerism on material life was earlier than previously assumed; for example, see Carole Shammas, The Pre-Industrial Consumer in England and America (Oxford: Clarendon Press, 1990); and Grant McCracken, Culture and Consumption: New Approaches to the Symbolic Character of Consumer Goods and Activities (Bloomington: Indiana University Press, 1988).

10 A good overall historical introduction is Edward Lucie-Smith, The Story of Craft: The Craftsman's Role in Society (Oxford: Phaidon, 1981).

11 For an introductory (although somewhat dated) bibliography of women's material culture, see the discussion by Francis A. de Caro in his Women and Folklore: A Bibliographic Survey (Westport: Greenwood 1983), 36-41.

In a broader sense, the person who fashioned the object was obviously creating lasting symbols of power and obligation. In the past, craft carried with it the necessity of obligation: the obligation to respond to the immediate demands of local customers and patrons. Today, the craftsperson's obligation is to the market, to capitalistic demands. We subject our creations to juries and competitions, often controlled by the elite powers of craft professionals.[12] Power has shifted from the local to the international contexts, from the user to the arbiters of taste. So craft becomes not simply utilitarian but a symbol of monetary power. We turn to art and craft investment advisers, in fact, who tell us what to buy, what will give a satisfactory return on our money. Purchases are weighed in terms of market return, not taste.

Or craft becomes a vehicle of power in the realm of leisure. Only certain classes have enough income (and leisure) to weave linen, spin wool, work wood, or turn a pot. Those groups that scribble on paper or speak at conferences or sit at desks behind computer screens turn to craft, while the so-called "working classes" (a truly accurate term?) may not be so eager to engage in or purchase what we consider to be crafts.[13] Craft increasingly becomes the playground of those with social and economic power, often the same power that persuades others to consume rather than create.

And finally, many of these issues centre on the question of identity. Why do crafts become a symbol of a group? Why do we turn to objects as our group identity symbols, rather than to attitudes or emotions or beliefs?[14] We make something, and somehow we connect ourselves as a nation. When we revive our crafts, we do so in the name of group identity, with little thought given, perhaps, to how changed the function of those objects really is. Is this beneficial? Does it not mean that objects are no longer considered aesthetically important, but are simply symbols for some other social issue? When

12 Issues such as the influence of juries, popular aesthetics, and marketing on craft traditions is discussed in Vlach and Bronner, Folk Art and Art Worlds, 195-266; and in the special issue of New York Folklore 12, no.1-2 (1986) dealing with marketing of folk art.

13 Traditional crafts are often seen not as rewarding but a chore to be endured until changing technologies and economics liberate the craftsperson from the necessity of making certain objects. For example, see Gerald L. Pocius, Textile Traditions of Eastern Newfoundland, Canadian Centre for Folk Culture Studies Paper 29 (Ottawa: National Museums of Canada, 1979), 61-66.

14 A good introduction to the question of identity and cultural symbols is Edward H. Spicer, "Persistent Cultural Systems: A Comparative Study of Identity Systems That Can Adapt to Contrasting Environments," Science 174 (1971): 795-800.

the object itself is less important than what it represents, how has the nature of craft changed?[15]

What about our identity as it is related to taste and aesthetics? Do we foster individual and collective identity through common or competing aesthetics? Neil Forrest urges craft practitioners to become agents of change. I see societies where the aesthetic awareness concerning crafts seems to be remarkably higher than our own: Scandinavia, for example, or the Baltic countries.[16] Identity, in a sense, for many of these places, comes from an awareness of and demand for crafted objects that meet aesthetic as well as functional needs. How do we produce a level of aesthetic awareness in our own culture, or should we?

How do we become agents of change? How do we foster a meaningful identity through crafts? By becoming arbiters of taste? By restricting craft through a network of experts, or by letting the market take its toll? The experts may prefer to keep craft objects in the circles where they are already found: that of the intellectual and economic elites. Can we convince the ordinary person that individual creativity and creation are possible, yet essentially say that only experts have the knowledge to design and build? (That is certainly not what we believe was done in the Middle Ages.) We still keep the crocheted toilet paper covers out of our craft fairs and galleries, and perhaps it is at the flea market down at the local mall where the more democratic craft is displayed. We worry about the morality that the art gallery world imposes on us, and then we impose our own morality on ordinary people who are creating objects that we label – ethnocentrically – as kitsch.[17]

In a world where craft has no common language, no common aesthetic, ultimately we do not use these objects to fashion our identity. If, with wealth, we all have unique craft objects in our day-to-day environments, we all wear different clothes, different jewellery – our shared aesthetic of difference – then what really creates our identity? The *other* objects of our shared language: whether it is a 2,000-square-foot or 3,000-square-foot house;

15 An excellent study of a craft revival is Charles L. Briggs, The Wood Carvers of Cordova, New Mexico: Social Dimensions of an Artistic "Revival" (Knoxville: University of Tennessee Press, 1980); see also his "The Role of Mexicano Artists and the Anglo Elite in the Emergence of a Contemporary Folk Art," in Vlach and Bronner, Folk Art and Art Worlds, 195-224.

16 For similar comments about Austria see Gloria Hickey, "A New Place for Ceramics", Ceramics Symposium, "Identity and Place of Specific Mediums in Contemporary Art Practice", Banff Centre for the Arts, Banff, Alberta, November, 1993, p.4.

17 I deal with the problem of such categories in relation to a specific Newfoundland craftsperson in Gerald L. Pocius, "Newfoundland Traditional Crafts: Types and Stereotypes," Artisan (Canadian Crafts Council) 4, no.5 (1981): 15-20.

whether a BMW or a Lexus; whether the holiday house is in southern France or in the Gatineaus.[18] Because we have broken with the common languages of our artifact past, we find it difficult to assert our identity through the shared aesthetics of idiosyncratic craft, and thus it may be becoming a less important symbolic vehicle in our modern world.

So the craft world I see today is somehow struggling to maintain links with some nostalgic past, but only with parts of that past, the parts that serve our need to fabricate roots in our rootless world. I see power arrangements, where gender issues still determine what is even considered under the rubric of craft. And power arrangements where arbiters of taste dictate what is aesthetically pleasing. And, in all this, we struggle with questions of identity: the identity of our professions, the identity of our gender, the identity of our nations. In this struggle, craft no longer is primarily that which is useful or pleasing, but objects that settle our uneasiness about who we are.

Each medieval villager knew their place as they sat in the cathedral, knew their place in the world. We placeless moderns turn to those other worlds (such as the cathedrals of the past or the sacred objects of other cultures) to invent our niches, our own identity.[19] But we must never deceive ourselves into thinking that the object was the only key to identity in those other times and places. For we often fail to see the restraints, duties, and, most important, the obligations that were the fundamental basis of these other craft worlds. Nor must we fail to realize that the most important values of these cultures had often nothing to do with things.

18 The importance of such new shard artifact symbols is discussed in Pierre Bourdieu, Distinction: A Social Critique of the Judgement of Taste, trans. Richard Nice (Cambridge: Harvard University Press, 1984); and Paul Fussel, Class: A Guide Through the American Status System (New York: Touchstone, 1992).

19 The condition of placelessness seems increasingly to be an issue of (post)modern life. I discuss this in my study of one Newfoundland community: A Place to Belong: Community Order and Everyday Space in Calvert, Newfoundland (Montreal: McGill-Queen's University Press; Athens: University of Georgia Press, 1991), especially chapter one and the concluding chapter.

Craft and the Museum

SandraFloodCarolMayerJohnVollmerMichelCheff

Sandra Flood

Contemporary Craft
Collecting in British Museums

Sandra Flood, for six years the editor

of the Saskatchewan Craft Council's journal,

The Craft Factor, is pursuing doctoral

research on the collection of contemporary

craft by Canadian museums.

Collection d'artisanat contemporain dans les musées britanniques

Cet article traite de certains aspects de la recherche effectuée en vue de l'obtention d'une maîtrise en 1993. Neuf collections d'artisanat contemporain multimédias, les politiques d'achat, l'historique et le contenu de ces collections ont été analysés et les conservateurs respectifs ont accordé une entrevue visant à explorer : les fondements sur lesquels s'appuient les décisions concernant le choix des oeuvres, les critères de sélection des pièces particulières et le niveau actuel de collection de l'artisanat contemporain (de 1950 à nos jours). Trois questions connexes concernaient l'emplacement de l'artisanat par rapport aux beaux-arts, aux arts décoratifs et aux objets ethnographiques; les aspects de la production artisanale contemporaine ne faisant pas l'objet de collection et les tendances intellectuelles sous-jacentes de l'artisanat. Des renseignements supplémentaires ont été apportés à partir de six collections et d'une entrevue avec l'un des conservateurs d'art contemporain.

Cet exposé démontre la difficulté de situer les collections d'artisanat contemporain, tout particulièrement celles relevant des arts décoratifs, l'absence de renseignements sur les collections et la surreprésentation des oeuvres de céramique. Les collections étudiées furent toutes montées dans les années 70, elles sont relativement petites et n'ont vraisemblablement pas, à l'exception d'un seul cas, fait l'objet d'une analyse contextuelle ou historiographique de l'artisanat au cours de leur formation. Cette recherche a identifié des différences prononcées entre le traitement réservé à l'artisanat contemporain dans les collections qui lui sont exclusivement réservées et dans les collections générales d'arts décoratifs qui s'expliquent principalement par les politiques (longueur et détail) et la connaissance des conservateurs.

On soutient qu'il existe un conflit inhérent entre les critères des oeuvres d'artisanat historique et ceux des oeuvres d'artisanat contemporain dans les collections d'arts décoratifs. On a appris que les critères utilisés dans le cadre des politiques sont le talent, le moyen d'expression, le type d'artisan (professionnel, éminent), l'historiographie et l'innovation. «L'excellence esthétique» n'a constitué une préoccupation que dans un seul cas. L'artisanat n'a pas été défini. Les achats sont influencés par les considérations d'ordre budgétaire (restrictions et instabilité à l'heure actuelle), l'état des lieux, la dynamique interne de la collection et par le conservateur. Les conservateurs, exerçant semble-t-il une influence importante, n'ont pas toujours les connaissances adéquates, et ils peuvent se désintéresser et se servir en grande partie d'une série de critères de sélection tendant à démontrer que la personnalité du conservateur (un domaine inexploré) joue un rôle considérable dans la stratégie globale et la sélection de pièces particulières. L'auditoire, lorsqu'on en a tenu compte, était perçu comme une élite de connaisseurs.

Cet article prétend que les collections d'artisanat contemporain reflètent la professionalisation de l'artisanat, sont fondées sur une théorie moderniste non exprimée et sont contrôlées par l'artisanat d'élite. Ceci déforme la définition de l'artisanat et affecte la présentation, la collection et l'interprétation.

In my research for my master's degree, I looked at nine multi-media contemporary craft collections, their acquisitions policies, and the history and contents of the related collections; and interviewed their curators in order to examine the basis on which decisions as to what to collect are made, the criteria by which individual pieces are selected, and the amount of contemporary craft (1950 to the present) that is being collected. Three related questions were the museum's location of "craft" in relation to fine art, applied art, and ethnographic objects; aspects of contemporary craft production not being collected; and the intellectual directions underlying craft. I received information from six other craft collections, and I also interviewed a curator of contemporary art in order to identify possible differences. A survey of this size may not seem large enough to give reliable findings, but since the collections covered a wide range of variables in status, scale, funding, and focus and included two of the three "core" collections, they can be considered representative.

In view of the fact that my external examiner saw the dissertation as a "howl of anguish," I would at this point like to acknowledge gratefully the curators who fitted my interviews into their busy schedules and to say that, despite everything that follows, there are some brilliant collections being put together under discouraging conditions.

The first problem was that it was difficult to find contemporary craft collections unless they were labelled as such. Applied arts collections may or may not collect contemporary work; "textiles" may or may not include contemporary textiles. The British Crafts Council is currently researching a location list. Curators seemed hardly better informed than I was, tending to say, "We tend to know such and such may collect crafts but may not know specifics." They seemed to have little contact with other craft curators, although curators of craft collections tended to be more actively interested in and knowledgeable about other craft collections than curators of applied art collections containing contemporary craft. It was a problem not only to find collections but to find out what was in them, particularly as only a small proportion of work may be on display. Four out of ten had current handouts listing works in their collection, two had partial lists; none had catalogues.

Of 63 collections identified, I had information about the media in 47. Of these, 43 collect ceramics, 13 of these collect only ceramics, and 8 collect ceramics and one other medium. This does not reflect the level of ceramics production in relation to other media according to the Crafts Council's Index of Craftspersons or the list of Scottish craft businesses in Cultural Trends. Of the remainder, 21 collect "textiles," 19 "glass," 16 "wood" including furniture, 15 jewellery and 15 "metal," 8 "paper," bookbinding, or calligraphy, and 7 "other." Four of these are single-medium collections.

The nine collections all opened in the 1970s and are quite small: four contained from 50 to 190 works, the two largest contained approximately 500 and 1,020 pieces. The reported reasons for the establishment of the collections were varied: to record and study twentieth-century craft makers and history; to promote and exhibit new craft; to maintain or revive traditional skills; to demonstrate the continuity of craft traditions; to give a location a distinct identity; as a result of additional gallery space through new building; and as a lever to acquire recognition of craft through representation as a distinct entity in a major museum. For the most part there is little evidence of a well-thought-out contextual or historiographical analysis of craft as a foundation for most of these collections. Lacking this, the curators used medium as a first basis of selection: that is, the criterion for acquisition was whether the medium was considered to be a craft or applied-art medium.

The acquisitions policies referring to craft ranged in length from a sentence to six pages. Where crafts were part of an applied-art collection, there was either no specific policy for craft or it was mentioned briefly and usually seen as a continuation of the historical collection. Craft collections tended to have longer, more detailed policies, giving as criteria: technical excellence and skilled use of materials; the type of maker – "artist crafts-people," professional, acclaimed; historiography – "to record and show the history of the British Crafts Movement"; and innovation. "Aesthetic excellence" was mentioned only once. Common to both sets of policies was a geographical restriction; that is, the maker or artifact had to have a local connection, and/or the maker must be British by birth or domicile. This latter requirement was sometimes in conflict with the criteria for maker, with the result that occasionally graduate students, production makers, or amateurs were allowed in. "Craft" was not defined in any policy.

Within the collection, acquisitions appear to be influenced by four things: budget, the institution's physical and conceptual restrictions, the internal dynamic of the collection, and the curator's schemata. Seven of the collections belong to "local authorities" (that is, municipal or local governments) and are dependent on them for funding, which in the current political situation is unpredictable and rapidly decreasing. In addition, only one had a specific craft acquisitions budget of a named amount; others worked with undefined budgets or were in competition with other departments where both historical objects or fine arts were seen to have priority. One collection was funded directly by the government as a national organization and has by far the largest annual budget. One collection was a charitable trust relying heavily on donations and bequests and buys "in a very small way" using part of the interest from an endowment fund. Four are currently not collecting (two have no acquisitions budget), three are collecting on a very small scale, and two are collecting vigorously on comparatively restricted budgets. The instability of local authorities also raised questions, not just about current collecting, but about the continued existence of collections. There are in Britain an estimated thirty to forty private collectors building collections on a museum scale, and some of these have collected three or four specific makers over a long period – something no collection I saw had managed to do – but "somebody is not going to hand over their life collection to a local authority [museum]" under present conditions.

The physical conditions imposed by the institution relate to display space, storage space, environmental conditions, and conservation. Inadequate display (and storage) space is the reason given most often for not collecting furniture and large textiles. In some cases "the... size of an object was determined by the size of the display cases." Fragility and the short life of some materials were a consideration; and in one case "purchases were affected by the attitude of the conservation department" – a comment that indicated some conflict. In addition, exhibiting and the scale of the building impose considerations of scale and "presence." I will discuss the conceptual conditions imposed by the institution later.

The internal dynamic of the collection leads to decisions made on the basis of apparent gaps: in makers, "fairly major names I felt should have been in there"; or media "major developments"; or techniques, "variety"; or work from particular periods.

By "curator's schemata" I mean the curator's concept of the collection within the confines of the policy. Given that many policies were vague and confused, the curator was seen as a major force in the defining and vitality of the collection. A high level of interest is assumed in craft curators; however, that may not be true of applied-art curators. How much a lack of interest may be due to lack of confidence and knowledge about craft is an open question, but curatorial interest is essential to the viability of the collection, and lack of interest accounted for the decline or stasis of at least two of the collections.

In the light of the Crafts Council's lament in 1985 (which had not changed by 1992) that "museum staff were rarely trained in the crafts and often did not know how to approach them," I looked at the education of the curators. Craft curators tended to have practical craft education and experience; applied-arts curators did not. This has implications for the selection and assessment of works in an area where the selection policies concentrated on the skilled use of materials and techniques and innovation as criteria for selection. The assessment of technical difficulty comes from accepted standards and a specialist body of knowledge, but only three curators openly expressed confidence in their ability to assess technique, and five did not consider it of primary importance. Beyond this relatively objective area, curator's criteria were unformulated and assumed to be self-explanatory. Only one curator had a personal check list of criteria and a definition of "excellence." Six curators assessed excellence by "gut reaction" or "instinct." While knowledge, experience, and a good "eye" played a part in the selection criteria, personality played a considerable part both in overall strategy and in individual selections. The influence of personality in the selection process has been little explored. Its effect on the collection appears to be accepted by curators without analysis.

I would like now to go back to the definition of craft, because this definition is the key to much of what is happening and will answer my last three questions. The assumption that they know what craft is is so deeply rooted that neither the museums in their policies nor I in my questionnaire saw a need to define it. This is also characteristic of much of the literature. The museum's definition is by inference and default. Like the commonly accepted definition, policies emphasized skill but did not define "art" and "handwork," although definitions were articulated by curators. Beyond this commonly accepted point there are further museum refinements: the requirement for "innovation" and "ingenuity"; the maker as professional, recognized, major, a designer-maker, making "an individual statement"; appealing to an "informed" group, an "elite, knowledgeable audience." What is being described is elite craft (artcraft); yet contemporary craft in fact covers a wide variety of practices and expressions, ranging from functional and domestic to gallery and conceptual, from handmade to CADCAM, from one of a kind to serially produced, from traditional to innovative, from one-person studio to co-operative group or workshop, from professional to amateur, from elite craft to folk craft and popular craft.

It appears that what is being recorded is a professionalization of craft due in part to the huge increase in the number of graduates from art colleges since the 1960s, graduates who train with painters and sculptors and want for themselves what the fine-art world offers in economic rewards and prestige, and who have in common, modernist discourses. Sue Rowley, an Australian theorist, argues that modernist "craftswriters and art critics alike sought to differentiate crafts from art by opposing the intellectual drive behind modern art to the intuitive, emotional, non-rational and experiential commitment of the crafts" and intensified the art/craft division. This theoretical division would account for the separatist location of craft within the museum as a "craft collection" and for the collection criteria of skill, technique, media, which with form, function, decoration, and style, Rowley argues, constitute a matrix of key words which map out the critical discourse of modernist crafts. The predominance of "showcase" exhibitions where the work is left to speak for itself with little or no textual or contextual information is an outcome of this alignment with fine art. The possibility that modernist theory (or any other) might underlie their collecting and exhibiting strategies was at no time mentioned by the curators.

In these nine collections, elite craft was in only one instance located with fine art (they happened to be in the same room), and that was in an institution which had three possible locations: with fine art, as a discrete collection, and in an applied art collection. Contemporary craft was associated with applied art by medium, function, or apparent historical relationship. The selection criterion for craft, however, was different and more limited than that for applied art, and applied art curators appeared to have difficulty relating it to their collections, explaining that contemporary craft was no longer "functional" and had lost its "raison d'être." Contemporary craft was separated from folk craft, which appeared to be seen as rural and defunct, a view that reinforces the impression of contemporary craft as divorced from traditional (and working-class) practices. Craft was also separated from ethnological objects, because they were seen as "cultural rather than craft objects," an opinion that denies both that ethnographic objects can also be craft objects and that craft objects – elite as well as folk and popular – have cultural connotations. Where "art" depends on being seen as "immediately powerful," it stands opposed to culture, which is historically and culturally contextualized. This may also explain the almost total lack of archival and contextual material being collected, except in the one collection set up for that purpose.

Time will not let me expand on the institutional dynamics of the museums and their influence on craft collecting. Since the democratization of museums, influenced by the French Revolution, they have teetered uneasily between remaining elite temples of arts and knowledge and becoming instruments for the education of the masses. The slide towards collected craft as that which is done by professional artists (and a rather limited group at that) rather than the general activity of a whole culture could leave museums open to public suspicion that the specific tastes of a class or profession are being generalized into an official definition of craft, in the process distorting and misrepresenting it and excluding an increasing number of craftmakers, both professional and amateur.

Bibliography

Ioannou, Noris, ed. 1992. *Craft in Society: An Anthology of Perspectives*. Fremantle, Australia: Fremantle Arts Centre Press.

Pearce, Susan M., ed. 1989. *Museum Studies in Material Culture*. Washington, D.C.: Smithsonian Institution Press.

Carol E. Mayer

"We Have These Ways of Seeing": A Study of Objects in Differing Realities

Carol E. Mayer is Curator of

Ethnology/Ceramics at the University

of British Columbia Museum of

Anthropology in Vancouver.

Ces manières de voir qui nous sont propres

Cet article étudie les déplacements parcourus par les objets, du fabricant au musée, et suggère que ceux-ci s'arrêtent dans des réalités construites divergentes dans lesquelles ils sont remis en contexte et renommés. On soutient que ces objets, une fois au musée, sont déplacés de l'état utile à l'état in-utile, leur historie est rédigée et ils sont placés dans un décor idéalisé construit selon des objectifs formels que le musée considère convenables et durables. Cet article recherche un attribut de temps, d'espace et d'objet qui permet aux gens de faire l'expérience d'objets qui passent de cet état distant, immobile et contenu à un état rapproché, dynamique et dégagé.

This paper investigates how the process of curating a new permanent exhibition of historic European ceramics at the Museum of Anthropology (MOA) at the University of British Columbia changed the way I think about objects and the role of exhibitions. As I looked at the different realities that objects pass through on their way to museums and investigated how they are viewed and renamed, this personal curatorial journey led me to ask why we do what we do and then to contemplate the consequences of how we answer these questions. In the tradition of anthropological inquiry this paper will explore these questions through "the idiosyncrasies of a single case" (Ames 1986, 12): one person's collection displayed in a single gallery. The collection is idiosyncratic in that it does not fit easily into the public or academic idea of what is suitable for exhibition in a museum of anthropology. It consists of historic ceramics made by cultures not addressed at MOA, the uncomfortably close-to-home "self," rather than the comfortably distant "other."

The displaying of objects is the one thing that unifies all museums; but how we display them and what we say about them demonstrates our separateness. By being organized and interpreted according to formalized objectives considered by the museum to be appropriate and enduring, objects in an anthropology museum help create an artificial representation of a particular past (Cannizzo 1987), an idealized landscape, constructed because "we see the world the way we do not because that is the way it is but because we have these ways of seeing" (Wittgenstein quoted in McGrane 1989, ix). We may think exhibitions provide correct "ways of seeing," but if the visitor chooses to ignore them or does not understand them, then he or she is left with the task of constructing meanings that may or may not run parallel with the ways of seeing of the creator of the object, the collector, or the curator.

As a curator I have developed a personal way of seeing that I have found useful when working with objects. It is based on the concept that objects, studied within an anthropological context, exist in at least three historically and often geographically distinct realities in which the use of different criteria attaches different meanings and names to them. In the first reality, that of the maker, the objects are manufactured in response to cultural requirements and are an integral part of the physical articulation of cultural processes. The second reality is that of the collector who chooses objects, often by type, and removes them from their intended context, treating them as commodities to be bought, sold, renamed as art or craft, and evaluated according to the tenets of connoisseurship and the surrounding art market. When the collector, for a number of reasons, transfers his collection to the third reality, the museum, the objects are renamed again according to a constructed classification system which prioritizes function. Here they are either stored in a private space or displayed in a public space. At MOA the storage (private) space is public so all the collection, with the exception of physically or spiritually sensitive material, is accessible to the visitor. Obviously, thinking about objects existing in differing realities is not a concrete construct, but is a useful device which has, for me, generated alternative ways of seeing.

I have always found the fairy tale of Sleeping Beauty an interesting analogy when thinking about the lives of objects: when she awoke after one hundred years, the world around Sleeping Beauty must have changed considerably, but the fairy tale leaves her in her castle to live happily ever after. Museums build castles, artificial reconstructions of a particular past, whilst ignoring the "sleeping" time of the objects, when they travelled in the world of their "other" – where they were reconsidered, re-evaluated, and renamed. Why collectors "saved," "rescued," or "valued" these objects during their second reality, their sleeping time, is seldom asked, and collectors are relegated to the acquisition file or the archives, viewed as stereotypes and left to fade away (Halpin 1990, 1). The museum staff decides which aspects of an object's existence are to be validated and remembered.

At the time of the planning and research for the new gallery at the MOA, the ceramics collection was still in the possession of the collector, Dr. Walter Koerner. This was an extremely unusual situation that offered a rare opportunity to get to know the collection, in its second reality, and the collector, while both were unencumbered with museum classification and naming systems. The collection contains approximately six hundred examples of southern, central, and western European ceramics ranging in date from the late fifteenth to the early nineteenth century. Three main ceramic traditions and technologies are well represented: tin-glaze earthenware, lead-glaze earthenware modelled in high relief, and stoneware. Since I knew that all the collection was to be displayed, curatorial editing was not an issue; the challenge was how to develop an organizing principle which encompassed the museum's mandate and the collector's rationale within an accessible "storyline."

Koerner's comments about his collection were couched in the language of the connoisseur: "This is a good piece," "This is very rare," "The Metropolitan has one of these," "There are only two of these in the world." At first, he seemed to be a typical decorative arts collector, looking for age, rarity, skill, and aesthetic quality in objects that were detached from their functional purpose and organized into collector's categories. This seemed to suggest a straightforward organizing principle. However, on closer inspection he seemed to purchase indiscriminately, because, alongside wares which conformed to models of connoisseurship, there were pieces he referred to as "crockery." Some pieces were obviously valuable and others were not, so desirability and price were not necessarily synonymous. The organizing principle started to look more complicated. One thing was clear: he constantly singled out some pieces for visual attention and others for gentle handling.

First impressions are always important as are the words one uses when trying to record them. During the research phase I noted the expressions Koerner used when he talked about his collection, and I used his words as cues when thinking about the development of an organizing principle. It is a humbling experience to look back at the words I used to describe the collection once it had been transferred to the museum: "unique wares that were vehicles for the most sophisticated and up-to-the minute artistry; carefully controlled wares that were made according to specific sets of rules; vibrant naive wares dashed off with a sure hand for the popular market – a range seldom found in museum holdings." We have these ways of seeing. Once Koerner and I ventured beyond descriptive language it became clear that he "curated" his collection within a social historical framework, using the sixteenth- to eighteenth-century Anabaptist wares as the centre from which almost everything else radiated. These wares were, to him, symbolic of the power of the beliefs of the Anabaptists: once those beliefs were eroded by the existing religious establishment, the rules of manufacture relaxed significantly and the ceramics lost their purity of form and decoration and were renamed folk art. By collecting the earlier, "purer" ceramics, at a time when they were virtually ignored by other collectors, Koerner has guaranteed that the power of the Anabaptist beliefs, as they were symbolized, for him, in their ceramics, will not be forgotten. This desire to "rescue" objects made by cultures under pressure to assimilate had much to do with his own personal history. The question posed for Koerner and me was whether any of this should be included in the exhibition.

Even though it was clear that the Anabaptists were the main focus for Koerner, he also had an impressive collection of lead-glazed high-relief tiles. There was not a clear connection between his tile collection and the curatorial rationale for his tin-glaze wares, but the existence of the tiles made him a "multiple collector." He always insisted that he "just like[d] them." When asked why he collected stove tiles (Hafner ware), he responded, "I like nice things, they are beautiful and rare... my love for tiles has nothing to do with price." In his home he had many of them framed as individual pieces of art, even though the maker had intended them to be parts of a large architectural structure – a stove. The tiles are displayed as art in the new gallery and a stove is shown to provide the context: the original stove had been broken apart so that the tiles could be sold as separate pieces of art. Given my penchant for associating objects with their different realities, it can be said that the museum put these individual tiles, which were being guided towards their second reality (the art market), back into their first reality (a functional stove, as the maker intended), and then presented the reconstruction in a third reality (in its museum interpretation), thus providing a context for the existing deconstructed tiles already settled in their second reality (as art objects). We have these ways of seeing.

The transition from the second reality to the third was greeted with confusion, opposition, and delight. When the collection came to the museum, the question posed was "What is that stuff doing in a museum of anthropology?" (see Mayer 1992). It was answered, but not yet with great conviction, by posing another question: "Why shouldn't anthropology museums embrace Europeans and move beyond studying the 'other'?" This was qualified with the reasoning that anthropologists do claim to study all humankind – so bringing Europeans into the framework could facilitate the beginning of anthropologizing "self." Even, "Is this not an opportunity to be more honest, less authoritative, perhaps even to confront issues relating to racism and exclusion with action rather than rhetoric?" Or did it have something to do with the relationship of the collector with the MOA?

Certainly the museum likes to view and promote itself as a common ground for sharing ideas: there is theoretical agreement with the current tendency which advocates desanctifying works of art and promoting the contemporary museum as an "instrument to democratize culture" (Herreman 1989, 197). Yet this theoretical agreement about the concept of sharing is not easy for those who still believe that museums should serve as "dignified repositories for symbols and icons of days gone by" (Vonier 1988, 27). It seems that time spent on democratizing the museum is being met with some success, but perhaps success would be more assured if more time were spent on democratizing those who work in museums. At MOA the Koerner collection is displayed in accordance with a philosophy of accessibility: everything is shown. There is no doubt, however, that the display techniques used in the new gallery encourage the visitor to view the collection as art, and the space is grand enough to suggest to some that the ceramics are special, chosen, sanctified. Recent surveys have shown that most visitors are unaware of any underlying ordering principles, nor do they question the collection's presence in a museum of anthropology. Working with the Koerner collection in its second reality accentuated, for me, the idea that choices made by those inside a museum, when organizing an exhibition, are guided by the collection perimeters determined by seldom understood outside rationales: collectors construct collections out of what remain separate pieces, and the pieces are placed in created categories which together form a single entity. Once moved to the museum, this entity may disappear. The question is "Should it?"

One thing that does disappear once a collection is moved to a museum is the tactile connection between the collector and the collection. Once documented, the collection is seldom touched and never used. The useful arts are rendered "use-less," and, as Pomian has so effectively stated, nobody is slain by the swords, cannons, and guns on display in the military museum, and not one single worker or peasant uses the utensils, tools, and costumes assembled in folklore collections or museums. The same is true of everything which ends up in this strange world where the word "usefulness" seems never to have been heard of, for to say that the objects which now await only the gaze of the curious were still of some use would be a gross distortion of the English language. The locks and keys no longer secure any door, the machines produce nothing, and the clocks and watches are certainly not expected to give the precise time of day (Pomian 1990, 7).

Reading Pomian, I reflected on the writing of Natzler, who talks about handling a pot to discover its personal and endearing nature, and Bernard Leach, who views the beauty of ceramic form as being both subjective and objective: "It is subjective in that the innate character of the potter, his stock and his tradition live afresh in his work; objective in so far as his selection is drawn from the background of universal human experience" (Leach 1976, 20). I also watched the film *Utz,* which tells the story of a collector of Meissen porcelain. In one candle-lit scene Utz sits surrounded by his collection; he touches and handles a few selected figurines, and as his gaze intensifies, so does his passion, and the figures, for him, come to life and dance. I also read the book *Utz,* where, in stark contrast to the film, the collector articulates his feelings about objects in museums:

> An object in a museum case must suffer the denatured existence of an animal in the zoo. In any museum the object dies of suffocation and the public gaze – whereas private ownership confers on the owner the right and need to touch. As a young child will reach out to handle the thing it names, so the passionate collector, his eye in har-

Hawk Olla, 1990
by Laura Wee Lay Laq
ceramic vessel

Tapestry, 1990
by Ruth Jones, French Dinner Service by
unknown artist, eighteenth century

Plate, 1993
by Gillian McMillan

mony with his hand, restores to the object the life-giving touch of its maker. The collector's enemy is the museum curator... Ideally, museums should be looted every 50 years, and their collections returned to circulation. (Chatwin Bruce 1989)

Consideration initially turned towards recognizing the historical value of the collection and then its relevance in this time and space: to question where it fits within the current frames of reference. As Tam Irving has pointed out in his introduction to the exhibition "Choosing Clay," the "roots of ceramic tradition still play a dominant role insofar as the vessel occupies a central position either as functional entity or metaphorical referent." He goes on to say, "These artists are not concerned with innovation but prefer, like classical musicians, to reinterpret established themes."

The recontextualizing of past philosophies within the framework of contemporary material culture is a phenomenon which can be traced back to the Romans, who, in the second century BC adopted the classicism of what was Greece by removing and copying the material object which embodied that classicism. The artists of the Renaissance followed suit, as did the Victorians. In the time and space we are currently occupying, new objects are being created, unique to their maker, but containing echoes of these different realities which exist in our "conscious or subconscious selves" (Ames 1992, 141). How can we articulate these connections between historic and contemporary ceramics without marginalizing either of them? Could this be an important role for the Koerner collection?

It occurred to me that if the collector's need to handle and gaze was so intense, then perhaps this was something we could make available to the contemporary potter. Perhaps they too could make contact with the historical artist or potter. "In a broad way the difference between the old potters and the new is between unconsciousness within a single culture and individual consciousness of all cultures" (Leach 1976, 20). These thoughts initially encouraged me to include some contemporary work in the gallery. One hand-built and burnished vessel made in 1990 by a Vancouver artist, Laura Wee Lay Laq, was displayed opposite a wheel-thrown and glazed vessel made in about 1590. They share a simplicity of form; yet the technology used to create the newer piece predates the technology of the older piece by hundreds of years. By collapsing time the two pieces could converse with each other in the same space, yet remain strong enough to retain their individuality. Laura Wee Lay Laq refers to herself as an artist, and her work has been labelled "art" and has been shown in art galleries. Is it still "art" in an anthropology museum? If being singled out and lit artistically is enough to make it qualify, then it certainly is displayed as art. The older vessel is utilitarian in form but, it can be argued, shares a similar aesthetic, and it is displayed exactly the same way as Wee Lay Laq's piece. One difference lies in the identity of the artist – one known and one unknown – and another in the naming of the pieces: Wee Lay Laq's piece is called the *Hawk Olla;* during its life to date, the older piece has been named in accordance with its known function. Auction catalogues, the bibles of the art market, refer to such pieces as "important European pottery," thus avoiding having to call them craft or art. The conscious displaying of this piece as art demonstrates the power of the curator and designer to rename.

Elsewhere in the gallery two contemporary weavings by Ruth Jones and May Smith are displayed alongside the ceramics that inspired them: one a flamboyant colourful tapestry woven in the Aubusson tradition and the other a plain, unpretentious blue and white weaving. A fourth artist, Gordon Miller, was asked to illustrate the glazing and painting process used on maiolica, and Ulrike Holbrueker recreated the moulding process used to manufacture stove tiles. Their works are also displayed close to the original pieces that inspired them. All these artists live and work in British Columbia. Once the gallery opened, a symposium was held which brought together the three realities: makers, collectors, and museum curators. However, whereas the collectors and museum curators talked about historic ceramics, the makers were contemporary and creating works for the present and future. What significance, if any, did the Koerner collection have for them? True, there were a few contemporary pieces displayed in the gallery which owed some of their inspiration to the historic ceramics but was this sufficient? Had we made a point without a point being made? During the symposium the cases were opened for the various delegates who wanted to examine individual pieces: it was clear that makers, collectors, and curators all shared the need to touch, to contact, to weigh, to articulate their opinions and feelings about the ceramics. It became apparent that the exhibition could serve as a vehicle of change: perhaps by bringing together in one space and time the three realities normally separated, it could influence, inspire, or inform contemporary artist potters.

In 1993 I taught a course, "Topics in World Ceramics," to students of the Ceramic Department at the Emily Carr College of Art and Design and used the museum's collection to examine the social, technical, and artistic history of ceramics – but mainly to let the students touch "the real thing." I know that the idea of students working directly with collections is not new, but it is one that has become lost somewhere in the museum's control mechanisms that protects objects from the touch of the uninitiated. These students had never touched historic pieces, and they were not really enthralled with the literary, academic, ethereal, untouchable world of the arts; what they want is to get in touch with their "ancestors." Their final project was to produce a contemporary piece for an exhibition which contained echoes of a technology, form, decorative technique, iconographic message, or whatever, found in the information I had shared with them, and of their personal and physical contact with the historical pieces. Joining the company of the maker, collector, and curator, the students touched, held, and examined the works made so long ago but existing in this reality for now. They were asked to consider the question posed so eloquently by Alan Caiger-Smith:

> What is it in a tradition that enables such feeling to come to the surface through what are, after all, mere lines and shapes painted on a simple glaze? Why does one piece have an inner content, whereas another, very similar, is only decorative? What is it that men pass down from one to another in a living tradition that makes that tradition more than the sum of its technical process and skills? (Caiger-Smith 1973, 80)

They thought about their own works in the future. How will they interact with works yet to be created? Will they be allowed to? Some students were inspired by earlier technologies:

> I decided to stray from the Greek firing method and use an electric kiln which maintains a strict oxidizing atmosphere. By doing this I hoped to gain more control over colours and simplify the firing procedure, although this sacrificed the ability to reproduce the rich black of the Greek potters. The designs on the pot are derived from standard designed uses on Classic pots. (Jay MacLennan, 1993)

With one student, the image on a poster triggered an idea which, when expressed in clay bore no apparent resemblance to its inspiration:

> This horse was inspired by a horse and knight vessel made during the time of the Silla kingdom in Korea (668-935 AD). I have chosen to ignore the original functional aspect and instead have chosen to concentrate on the use of animal imagery. My horse is a functional piece in a different sense. I like to think he makes people smile when they look at him, and that is a function. I like to think that people will see him

and maybe have a deeper understanding of who I am, and that is a function. It is also my wish to make a piece that looks like a toy that people want to pick up and handle. To give them a connection to the child within them, the naive, playful side of themselves that they may have lost touch with. That is what I hoped to accomplish with my piece. (Dale Mervyn, 1993)

Some were interested in specifically recognizing the role of the historical ceramic artist in relation to their own:

During the sixteenth century in Italy, artists painting on maiolica achieved more recognition than ceramic artists of any other time. Istoriato plates depicted not only mythical and biblical stories but also current events of significance to the artist. Using similar technology in clay, glaze and firings I sought to recreate a pope's hat plate but the decoration has become very much centred in this time. The images on this plate reflect my excitement in pursuing ceramic studies at the Emily Carr College of Art and Design. All the vessels depicted on the rim were made during the last year. In the central well sits the artist painting this plate. (Gillian McMillan, 1993)

This piece contains layers of personal iconographic messages which describe the world of the artist at the time she made the plate. Whether these messages will continue to accompany the piece is not known. Will the intent of the artist be recorded, and will it be compatible with the intent of the collector? And if the piece ends up in a museum, will these "intentions" be accessible to the curator?... and will he or she ignore them or incorporate them as part of the conversation about the piece? Will the piece be renamed by "others"? The students at Emily Carr College were asked to consider these questions when looking at historic pieces and how they are presented inside a museum or gallery, to consider how they felt when their own piece left their hands and became accessible to everybody, to consider how the words in their artist's statements could act as bridges between the object and viewer, to consider their piece in an anthropology museum where the "other" is dominant, and to consider the relationship between their piece and the "other."

Many potters will agree that their work is firmly rooted in the non-imitative re-interpretation of the history of ceramics. All things new owe some allegiance to the past, so it seems to be incomprehensible that barriers would be erected to separate these entities. The experience of working with the Koerner collection, intellectually, physically, and emotionally, enabled me to think not only about how objects function in differing realities, but also how past philosophies can be carried forward and incorporated in contemporary work. The European ceramics were presented within a framework conducive to the museum's ideology and included some maker's rationale, some collector's rationale, and some relevance to the contemporary scene. However, it was the contact with the objects initiated by the art school students two years after installation that actually raised the possibility of a fourth reality, a reality not contained in a chronological time or space, rather a reality that is a concatenation of the other three – perhaps an attribute of time, space, and object which releases, enriches, informs, and inspires creative expression while rising above the vicissitudes of language.

Given this direction, the debate about the inclusion of a European collection of ceramics in a museum of anthropology has, in my mind, become a border skirmish relegated to the edges of the discipline. I would rather argue that this collection is an addition which has initiated a much more important discussion about the consequences of asking why we do what we do. The work produced by the art school students convinced me that a reality could exist where historically defined distances between "self" and "other" could be bridged and objects could be contacted but not necessarily categorized. The first challenge for a museum will be whether or not to accept the possibility of a fourth reality. If accepted, the second challenge will be how to nurture its existence and give people the opportunity to experience the moving of objects from a state of being distanced, immobilized, and contained, to one of being close, mobilized, and released. As untouchable objects become touchable, they move from abstract to concrete and are released from the constraints of the third reality – the museum. This is not how the world is at this time, but it could be – because we have these ways of seeing.

(I would like to thank Michael Ames, Marjorie Halpin, Tam Irving, and Ken Mayer for their comments on the draft of this paper.)

Bibliography

Alsop, J. 1982. *Rare Art Traditions: The History of Art Collecting and Its Linked Phenomena Wherever These Have Appeared*. New York: Harper and Row.

– – – 1978a. "Art History and Art." *Times Literary Supplement*, no. 3982 (July 28).

– – – 1978b. "Art Collection: The Renaissance and Antiquity." *Times Literary Supplement*, no. 3983 (August 4).

Ames, Michael M. 1986. *Museums, The Public and Anthropology*. Vancouver: University of British Columbia Press.

– – – 1992. *Cannibal Tours and Glass Boxes*. Vancouver: University of British Columbia Press.

Caiger-Smith, A. 1973. *Tin-Glaze Pottery in Europe and the Islamic World*. London: Faber & Faber.

Cannizzo, Jeanne. 1987. "How Sweet It Is: Cultural Politics in Barbados." *Muse,* Winter. (Canadian Museums Association), 22-27.

Chatwin, Bruce, 1989. *Utz.* New York: Penguin.

Csikszentmihalyi, Mihaly, and Eugene Rochberg-Halton. 1987. *The Meaning of Things: Domestic Symbols and the Self.* Cambridge: Cambridge University Press.

Duncan, Carol, and Alan Wallach. 1980. "The Universal Survey Museum." *Art History* 3, no. 4: 448-73.

Hainard, Jacques, 1983. "Collections Passion." *Museum* 35, no. 3: 157-58.

Halpin, Marjorie M. 1990. *Fragments: Reflections on Collecting.* Vancouver: UBC Museum of Anthropology Note No. 31. Vancouver: The Museum.

Herreman Yani, 1989. "A New Canvas for New Creative Talent: Contemporary Trends in Museum Architecture." *Museum* (Unesco) 41, no. 4: 196-200.

Irving, Tam. 1991. Introduction, in *Choosing Clay.* Vancouver: The Canadian Craft Museum.

Koerner, Walter C. 1988. *The Tree May Prefer Calm, But the Wind Will Never Subside.* Vancouver: n.p.

Leach, Bernard. 1976. *A Potter's Book.* London: Faber & Faber.

Mayer, Carol. 1992. "What Is That Stuff Doing in a Museum of Anthropology?" *Muse* 7, no. 3: 22-25.

McGrain, Bernard. 1989. *Beyond Anthropology: Society and the Other.* New York: Columbia University Press.

Montaner, Josep, and Jordi Oliveras. 1986. *The Museums of the Last Generation.* Academy Editions. London: St. Martin's.

Pomian, Krzysztof. 1990. *Collectors and Curiosities: Paris and Venice, 1500-1800.* Cambridge: Polity.

Rice, Prudence M. 1987. *Pottery Analysis: A Sourcebook.* Chicago: University of Chicago Press.

Sinopoli, Carla M. 1991. *Approaches to Archaeological Ceramics.* New York: Plenum.

Wilson, Timothy. 1987. *Ceramic Art of the Italian Renaissance.* London: British Museum.

Wittlin, Alma S. 1970. *Museums: In Search of a Usable Future.* Cambridge, Mass.: M.I.T. Press.

John E. Vollmer

Encounters with Narrative

John E. Vollmer is a museum consultant and
freelance curator who has organized exhibitions for
the Royal Ontario Museum, the Bata Shoe
Museum, and the Glenbow Museum, among others.

Artisanat – Rencontres avec la narration

Cet article examine comment et pourquoi l'artisanat s'exprime au moyen d'une série d'études de cas.

Pendant vingt-cinq ans, j'ai animé des interactions entre les objets et les gens dans le contexte interprétatif des expositions. Au cours de ces événements sociaux, on s'attend à ce que les objets communiquent. Malgré les efforts pour placer l'objet dans son contexte, souvent à l'aide d'un texte écrit, le dialogue tant souhaité par les conservateurs de musées et les éducateurs n'a souvent pas lieu. De manière répétée, les résultats des sondages indiquent que les visiteurs se rendent au musée, regardent, lisent parfois avant de quitter le musée, perplexes, déçus et ennuyés, ou, au contraire, s'ils manifestent une réaction positive, elle est souvent liée à leur appréciation du café, du magasin ou de la salle de toilettes.

Les objets artisanaux constituent l'exception à cette généralisation. Lorsqu'ils sont exposés, leur attrait provoque une réaction. Ce phénomène a été attribué aux qualités tactiles du travail artisanal (l'école d'appréciation du toucher), à son caractère fonctionnel (l'approche marxiste) ou à sa pureté esthétique (l'utilisation légitime des matériaux). Ces raisons ne suffisent pas à expliquer pourquoi l'objet d'artisanat contemporain communique.

Les objets lient le créateur et le spectateur. Dans le cas des objets faits à la main, ces liens sont particulièrement forts, minimisant ainsi la distance entre l'action humaine de créer et celle de faire l'expérience de l'objet créé. Ce lien n'est pas dialectique, il revêt plutôt un caractère narratif.

For twenty-five years I have staged interactions between objects and people within the interpretative contexts of exhibitions. At these public events, objects are expected to communicate. Despite efforts to contextualize the object, often by providing, among other things, a written text, the discourse that museum curators and educators seek often fails to occur. Repeatedly, surveys show us that visitors come, look, even read, and leave – confused, disappointed, and bored; or, if they react positively, they cite their experiences in the café, shop, or washrooms as factors that contributed to their pleasure.

In my experience, craft objects are exceptions to this generalization. On exhibition, their appeal evokes responses that are profoundly sensual and frequently sentimental. This phenomenon has been attributed to the tactile qualities of craft work (the touchy-feely school of appreciation), to functionality (the Marxist approach), or to aesthetic purity (the honest use of materials). Yet with the exception of the first of these, these are not the reasons overheard in galleries or in discussion for how or why these handmade objects communicate.

In fibre, as well as in other craft disciplines, objects link maker and viewer. Those links minimize the distance between the human actions of making and experiencing. The connection evokes narrative, rather than dialectical, relationships. In that way they challenge our ability to measure and quantify. Nonetheless it is in this narrative process that, I feel, we will find some of the meaning we seek in museum experiences.

In thinking about the issues raised by this paper, I have had to consider whether we do a disservice by lumping craft media together or trying to link things which are functional with those for which function has no relevance. I confess I don't have the answers; but those considerations, in addition to my own experience, make the following comments applicable to fibre only. Others will have to determine if any of these observations have validity for other media. For this discussion I would like to define fibre as ranging from paper to cloth and will include as well the many technical, manipulative, and embellishing strategies that are employed in their manufacture.

Since the mid-1940s we have witnessed a shift in thinking about what fibre making is all about. The requirement to make functional or useful objects has been joined by other criteria that focus on fibre-making processes as a means of expression in a context of art making. Some craftspersons have become fibre artists (although the term is less than satisfactory). For them, fibre-making techniques are viewed as strategies to be acquired and adapted. They attempt to fuse the physical act of making with the intellectual and emotional processes of expression. Conceptually such fibre objects are related to the concerns of mainstream art, yet their connection to the audience is frequently more direct and "meaningful" than that normally witnessed in mainstream art. One of the reasons for this distinction is, I feel, the role of narrative in the relationship between object and viewer.

Narrative, coming from the Latin *narrare,* to relate or make known, is defined by Webster as the art or practice of relating stories or accounts. It is in the intimacy of story telling that crafts engage an audience. In fibre we observe several elements of narrative on several levels: story and text, memory, association, imagination, projection, fantasy. Today I would like to discuss three broad considerations of narrative and a paradigm.

- First, for fibre objects, a kind of narrative *is implicit in the object itself.* Materials and techniques reveal the maker's mark – the result of hands controlling and shaping a sequence of actions and processes. We see the evidence for the passing of time both in discrete intervals and in a generalized sense. In this way the object creates a sense of time and space around it that encourages discourse.

- Second, subject matter that is part of the content of the piece or that is part of contextual images and ideas implied by a title can suggest an actual story. In other words, the maker gives us an *object with a text that can be read, literally or figuratively.* In a museological sense these objects carry their own interpretative labels.

- Third, narrative also occurs by association. By stimulating the memory of our personal and collective experiences, *objects involve viewers in story making.* Objects may arouse the imagination, leading to narratives based on projection and fantasy. In contrast to other narratives, these are personal and subjective and not controlled directly by the maker.

- And finally, a paradigm: behind any consideration of fibre is the paradigm embodying a relationship of fibre to human existence. It is omnipresent, tactile, and immediate. Humanity is central to the existence of fibre. It is this paradigm, I feel, that predisposes us to a narrative engagement with fibre. Let me expand on this idea briefly:

• The manipulation by the hand of various fibres can produce a thread or cord that forms an extension of the hand, becoming flexible tools that extend the human reach. Some examples are strings, cords, and ropes that become fish lines, nets, baskets, bags, or tumplines.

• Another dimension is characterized by the manipulation of threads or matting fibres to produce fabrics that become clothes, shelters, or even more sophisticated tools like sails. These extend the human body and expand the biosphere in which it exists. Some of these applications are functional; others are ornamental or charged with notions of identity, status, or affiliation.

• Thirdly, fibre can insulate, cushion, and nurture the human condition as bedding, draperies, and upholstery. Fabrics for the wall, floor, and ceiling enliven, comfort, and adorn private and public environments.

The following five case studies attempt to illustrate these points about narrative. The first is a historical example; the other are works by contemporary artists. Two work primarily within the two dimensions of the wall; the others approach their work three-dimensionally.

1. *The Joseph Quilt* (Royal Ontario Museum Collection, 956.151) was made by two members of Elmsley family from Woodstock, Ontario, in the late 1860s. It is an astounding demonstration of needlework. Few pass this type of object without acknowledging the commitment of time by its makers, in this case the grandmother and great-aunt of the donor. The museum catalogue notes a second quilt of the same subject that was "considered finer than this," also made by the same women for another member of the Elmsley family living in Caledonia.

Comments like "I can't believe anyone would spend that much time on a such an object!" recognize the painstaking skill that transformed one of the basic late-nineteenth century quilt-making techniques into a virtuoso display of personal artistry. Beyond this encounter with the narrative of technique is the actual Bible story of Joseph and his brothers that the makers have created in words and images. There is both a literal reading of the quilt surface and, for many viewers, the possibility of a broader reading based on their own knowledge of the Bible and religious upbringing.

Other forms of narrative can be detected in comments like "We use to have grandmother's quilt on the bed in the guest room"; "Victorian women's work! what a waste of time and effort"; and "Have you seen Jane Doe's quilts? She always making such lovely things." Such comments, which are usually made when there is more than one person looking at the object, illustrate some ways that the viewer brings personal knowledge, experience, or association to the crafted object.

Much of the literature about quilting suggests that the appeal of such objects is based on a direct link between the individual maker, the tradition it represents, and the present viewer, who is assumed to have had some experience with quilt making as a child. But in the latter part of the twentieth century, within the current multicultural population, such claims for the hold of nostalgia have little credence.

2. Although an object of a very different order, Jennifer Angus's appliqued, phototransfer, and beaded piece, *Flowery Tattooed Lady* (1992), exhibits similar narrative strategies. As in the case of the Ontario quilt, the maker's "marks" are an important element in establishing a link between maker and viewer. Although created as decorative piece for the wall, it plays upon connections to a variety of textile traditions that have at their basis some functional purpose. The intricacy and scale force the viewer to concentrate on the manipulation of elements that create the surface of the piece. The artist opens possibilities of interpretation through layering the specific techniques she has employed in the execution of the piece. Surface patterning is present in fact and referential guises – colour xerography, batik, beading, embroidery, and tattooing itself.

    Through figurative imagery, the viewer becomes aware of the artist's efforts to evoke a text. Angus implies a kind of biography for the woman whose photographic image (a kind of reality?) is framed by a Victorian exuberance of beaded Oriental-inspired foliage (a sort of imagination?) against a Southeast Asian batik fabric (a socio-political comment?). Each enriches narrative possibilities evolving from memory, projection, and fantasy.

3. Dorothy Caldwell's work is informed by the dyeing traditions of Japan and West Africa, yet is grounded in a keen awareness of her own geographical position. Resist and discharge processes, over-painting, and the manipulation of smaller elements are used repeatedly to produce dense layers of marks upon the surface. We are seldom able to sort out the

Flowery Tattooed Lady, 1992
by Jennifer Angus
Appliqué and photo transfer
Credit: Jeremy Jones

process in an orderly or tidy fashion. Rather we are left with an impression of a sumptuous richness across the surface which shifts and changes as we examine it.

Caldwell's more recent work set up a formal dialogue between the field and ground on the one hand and the edge and border on the other. Like the makers of Afro-American quilts who create a visual tension between a largely plain centre field and the seemingly random pieced edges, she strives to make "a good cloth" from many diverse parts. She does not ask us to use the work, but to assimilate it emotionally and intellectually, challenging us to consider just what a a good cloth might be.

Caldwell's design strategy juxtaposes multiple images and layering to evoke a kind of mental odyssey that is placed in some location that is both perceived and imagined. References to the landscape are at times specific but seldom literal. The viewer is pulled in and through these map-like pieces to participate in an abstracted narrative that is fragmentary and disjointed. Story making may be more meditative than literal. Her pieces encourage simultaneity; nonetheless the work has much to say to us.

4. *Black Tulip* (Chalmers Collection, 1989) is an example of the sculptural work of Sarah Quinton. Technically it is based on basketry traditions, with specific reference to Japanese armour-making techniques. These monumental, often totemic, images address issues of tying, binding, and wrapping. The maker's marks are complex and repetitive, setting up a rigorously controlled polyphony of theme and counterpoint. The artist's juxtaposition of hard and soft surfaces (wood moulding and waxed lacing tapes) literally builds a framework onto which a discourse about other contrasts can be projected. The viewer is asked to become enmeshed in a narrative that can be characterized as polemic. These shield-like forms evoke both offence and defence, creating tensions between issues of aggression and protection, between exposure and security, between notions of the finite and particular and the infinite and general.

5. Kai Chan, like many contemporary makers, cuts across categories and media. Jeweller, sculptor, designer, craftsperson – each employs technical strategies from the fibre repertoire in the search for expression. As a result, the lines between categories of creation are blurred or left purposely ambiguous. *Block Valentino* (1992) can be placed on a table and viewed as a tiny, colourful sculpture. It can also function as a sort of

deluxe Chinese puzzle to be taken apart and reassembled. If the piece proves too difficult to put back together, it can be put on and worn as a one-of-a-kind costume accessory. In this way a viewer's perception of story telling is literally part of the maker's action of story making.

The playful, often lyrical, quality of Chan's work is, however, deceptive. The reduction of his constructions that use string and wood to the simplest actions involving a cord made of fibre — looping, wrapping, and threading — forces us into a deeper consideration of the relationship between the medium and the human. Chan's work has progressed from looping and wrapping techniques that apply fibre to pieces of wood to threading techniques in which the string and wood become a single, integrated unit. In each is some of the expressive power of the thread. At first glance the prodigious quantities of thread wrapped over twigs and branches in Rabbit Tales (1985) appears random and accidental; nonetheless the effect on the viewer is as calculated as that of Robert Sera's sheet metal sculpture.

Patterns of Life (1992) is part of an evolving series of constructions based on sequences of wooden elements threaded on a cord that is stretched between nails in a wall. The various wooden elements (assorted sticks, pieces of balsa wood, or more recently toothpicks) suggest mnemonic devices for a set of specific but unknowable events. They embody a notion of passage, technically in that the elements are literally passed along the thread, physically in the changes of light and shadow on the wall, and metaphorically as elements in a narrative.

This paper raises a number of questions:

- What role should museums and galleries play in presenting contemporary craft to the public?

- What are those of us who work within the programming activities of those institutions actually supposed to do?

- How can we foster an engagement between the object and the viewer?

I suggest that before any of these questions can be answered, it is imperative that we learn how to appreciate and understand the connections that exist between makers and viewers. This paper is an effort to articulate some of those linkages.

Michel V. Cheff – Répondant

Les métiers d'art et le musée

Michel V. Cheff est le directeur exécutif du

Winnipeg Art Gallery et le président de l'Association

des musées canadiens. M. Cheff se penche

à l'heure actuelle sur les aspects de la gestion et

met en oeuvre des stratégies devant

servir de modéles dans le milieu muséal.

Abstract

Have museums defined the profile of the craftsman in terms of skill and virtuosity, in terms of aesthetics, material, and technique? Are we speaking of craftspeople or of artists? When does craft become art? And when does art become craft?

The position of the artist-craftsperson is a difficult one in a world of collectors, shops, galleries, and museums. Howard S. Becker speaks about this briefly in his book Art Worlds (University of California Press, 1982). He says that the artist-craftsperson produces with no particular buyer in mind and expects his or her work to be marketed through the conventional apparatus of dealers and museums; the buyer exercises control by buying or refusing to buy. What Becker says of the art market is applicable to museums, which have the power to promote artist-craftspeople, not solely by collecting, but also by exhibiting.

Are art museums making artist-craftspeople into superstars? Is the availability of fine craft produced by the top artist-craftspeople, as well as the eagerness of artist-crafts- people to be in the art museum, a trend we must encourage or resist? Should the art museum solicit the making of fine crafts as well as organize exhibitions of fine craft as fine art, or should the art museum only react to what comes its way?

The answers do not lie with me or my art-museum colleagues. I think the answers are, in part, to be found from the artist-craftspeople themselves and in part from the public.

Nous venons d'entendre trois points de vue sur les métiers d'art et le musée. Chacune des communications présentait notre sujet de façon personnelle. L'intention et l'attention qu'ont apportés nos intervenants à la préparation de leur communication appuient le sérieux et l'importance du sujet à l'é-tude de cette table-ronde. Je souhaite très sincèrement remercier nos panélistes, Sandra Flood, Carol Mayer et John Vollmer. Ils ont tous les trois scrupuleusement livré la marchandise annoncée au programme. Il est en fait assez rare que tous les intervenants d'une même table-ronde soient aussi fidèles. Félicitations!

Je tenterai de faire ressortir quelques points saillants des trois interventions d'aujourd'hui et je souhaite ajouter un quatrième élément au débat.

Quatre fonctions principales du musée sont ressorties par rapport au domaine des métiers d'art. Ce sont la collection, la recherche, l'exposition et la communication.

Sandra Flood a examiné les influences et les paramètres de la dynamique ''institutionnelle sur le plan de la *collection* d'objets des métiers d'art. Elle a posé les questions *du pourquoi* et *du comment* collectionner. Son travail, mené en Grande-Bretagne, semble facilement s'adapter au Canada.

La *recherche* comme moyen d'identification et de définition des catégories ainsi qu'en tant qu'intermédiaire menant à l'exploration des frontières, nous a été exposée par Carol Mayer. Carol a aussi esquissé le concept de la contextualisation et de la recontextualisation des objets via l'exposition. Elle suggère organiser la fonction des objets en des «réalités de différenciation.»

Une 4e fonction muséale, celle de *la communication* et de *l'éducation* nous a été révélée par la démonstration très convaincante que nous en a fait John Vollmer. En effet sa perspective qui cherche à créer des liens entre les objets et le public est tout à fait pertinente au mandat de responsabilité publique du musée.

Vous saurez apprécier l'expérience et l'expertise de nos collègues. Il est intéressant de noter que la théorie se trouve au creuset de la pratique et en retour, la pratique vient alimenter la théorie.

Considérons, si vous le voulez bien, que la théorie et la pratique ont engendré un sens réel de passion chez chacun de nos intervenants. Sandra Flood agit telle une détective, elle est passionnée par l'enquête et en quelque sorte l'interrogation. Carol Mayer possède la vraie passion de la connaissance des objets, toutefois elle cherche la connaissance par le truchement des gens qui créent ou qui collectionnent les objets. Elle est passionnément engagée et nous encourage tous à l'être autant qu'elle. La passion de John Vollmer est celle de l'observateur, de celui qui écoute 'afin de mieux transmettre. Sa passion est nourrie par le sens qui émane des objets au moment même où il atteint le spectateur/récepteur. Sa passion est ravivée par la réponse *immédiate et spontanée* du spectateur qui donne un sens à l'objet.

La connaissance est commune à Flood, Mayer et Vollmer. C'est une connaissance soit scientifique et fondamentale, soit humaniste ou transmissible. Leurs connaissances participent au dépassement des frontières du monde des métiers d'art et du monde de la muséologie.

Je tiens à soulever de nouveau certaines des questions et des défis amenés par nos collègues :

1. Comment le musée peut-il vraiment encourager la communication entre l'objet et le visiteur? Comment le musée peut-il créer une ambiance propice à l'interaction entre les créateurs et les récepteurs d'objets? (Vollmer)

2. Pouvons-nous assurer l'intégrité de l'objet et de son message? L'intention de l'artiste sera-t-elle documentée et complice du collectionneur, individuel ou institutionnel? L'information sur les objets sert-elle de lien entre l'objet et le spectateur? (Mayer)

3. Les musées définissent-ils et influencent-ils les «paramètres officiels» des métiers d'art? Devons-nous chercher à contrer la tendance du collectionnement sélectif, tel que pratiqué par une minorité de spécialistes, et non pas en tant qu'activité pratiquée par toute une culture? (Flood)

Vous aurez certes des commentaires, des questions sur ces sujets. Avant d'engager le dialogue, permettez-moi d'ajouter à l'interrogation en cours. Je parlerai du statut du créateur de métiers d'art et du processus de décisions d'exposer ou non les métiers d'art au musée *d'art*.

Premièrement une question : Les musées ont-ils esquissé le profil de l'artisan-créateur : en ce qui a trait à son métier et à la virtuosité de son oeuvre, en termes d'esthétique, de technique et de matériau? Les musées s'adressent-ils à des artisans ou à des créateurs : quand le métier d'art devient-il l'art? Et à quel moment l'art devient-il *métier d'art*?

L'artisan-créateur se trouve en position difficile dans un monde composé de collectionneurs, de boutiques, de galeries et de musées. Howard S. Becker en parle dans son livre intitulé *Art Worlds* (University of California Press, 1982). Il nous raconte que l'artisan-créateur produit sans aucun «acheteur» en tête et s'attend à être mis en marché au sein du réseau traditionnel des marchands et des musées; l'acheteur exerce un contrôle en achetant ou en refusant d'acheter. Ce que Becker impute au marché de l'art s'applique au contrôle que possède le musée qui détient le pouvoir de mettre les artisans-créateurs en vedette, en collectionnant ou en exposant leurs oeuvres.

Cherchons à comprendre comment les musées d'art choisissent les expositions temporaires de métiers d'art dans le cadre de leur programmation. Au musée d'art, la programmation d'expositions est proposée selon des critères et des normes de beaux-arts. Les musées d'art sont principalement préoccupés par des questions de problématiques spécifiques à l'art en général et particulièrement à l'art contemporain. Les métiers d'art sont souvent perçus et inclus soit sur le plan de «l'artisanat», soit sur le plan du «design». La tradition, la fonction et l'esthétique des objets servent de critères de base relativement aux choix des expositions.

Dans plus d'un musée d'art, les arts décoratifs et les métiers d'art provenant des collections permanentes sont relégués en périphérie des galeries principales. Les expositions sont rarement traitées au même plan médiatique comme événements majeurs. Les expositions d'oeuvres d'artisans-créateurs contemporains présentent généralement des oeuvres plutôt sculpturales et picturales qui se distancient du concept de l'objet fonctionnel-traditionnel. Ce phénomène s'explique facilement (selon H. Becker) puisque les artistes ont depuis déjà quelques temps envahi le domaine des métiers d'art, modifiant ainsi les normes, changeant les critères et adaptant les styles d'une activité longtemps dominée par les maîtres-artisans et les artisans-créateurs. Survient alors une sorte de contamination, heureuse ou non, qui fonctionne dans les deux sens, des beaux-arts aux métiers d'art et vice-versa.

De nombreux artisans ont franchi le pas de l'artisanat pur à un métier modelé sur les beaux-arts. Les paramètres en sont renouvelés. Je vous donne deux exemples représentants les deux côtés de la médaille. Joyce Wieland d'un côte et Jim Thompson de l'autre.

Il en résulte une compétition entre artistes, artisans et artisans-créateurs qui cherchent à exposer dans l'enceinte prestigieuse et sacro-sainte du musée d'art. La concurrence est courante et parfois belliqueuse.

Questions

Les musées d'art transforment-ils les artisans-créateurs en «vedettes de l'art»? La disponibilité du produit «métier d'art» haut de gamme et l'empressement des artisans-créateurs à exposer au musée d'art semblent faire école. Cette tendance doit-elle être encouragée ou contrée par le musée d'art?

Le musée d'art doit-il activement encourager la fabrication d'objets des métiers d'art et doit-il organiser des expositions où des objets sont traités comme des oeuvres d'art? D'un autre côté le musée d'art doit-il tout simplement réagir à ce qu'on lui propose?

Ni mes collègues de musées d'art ni moi-même n'avons les vraies réponses. Je pense que ce sont les artistes et les artisans-créateurs ainsi que le public des musées qui possèdent les éléments de réponses nécessaires.

La parole est à vous.

M a r j o r i e   M .   H a l p i n

Symposium Summary:
Craft in Canada

Marjorie M. Halpin is Associate Professor

of Anthropology and Curator of Ethnology at the

University of British Columbia Museum of

Anthropology. Her specific research interests are

the arts and rituals of the native peoples of the

British Columbia coast, especially the Tsimshian.

Au tournant de ce XXIc siècle, au moment où les réalités deviennent virtuelles, que les mots remplacent les actes et que les corps ne sont plus que signes, penser en termes d'«artisanat» devient un acte de nature radicale ou d'inspiration sentimentale. Ces deux tendances étaient présentes au colloque. Elles coexistaient également à la fin du siècle dernier et c'est ce qui m'a amené, en réfléchissant au contenu de cet article, à m'inspirer de William Morris. Pendant au moins deux décennies, depuis 1877 jusqu'à sa mort survenue en 1896, Morris a enseigné la relation qu'entretenait l'artisan médiéval avec son œuvre. «Et j'affirme, sans crainte de me contredire, écrit-il (cité en langue anglaise dans Grennan, 1945, p. 71), qu'aucune ingéniosité humaine ne peut produire une telle œuvre sans que le plaisir ne se mêle à l'entreprise du cerveau qui l'a conçue et de la main qui l'a façonnée.»[1] Il dit également de l'artisan dans The Aims of Art (cité dans le même ouvrage) «pauvre diable, la valeur de son œuvre était si insignifiante qu'il pouvait, des heures durant, la parfaire, pour son contentement et pour celui des autres.»[2] Les thèmes du plaisir dans l'accomplissement de l'œuvre et de la banalisation de celle-ci, exploités par Morris, font encore écho de nos jours. Toutefois, nous comprenons maintenant qu'il s'agit là des deux côtés d'une même médaille, dans une culture patriarcale

1 Traduction libre
2 Traduction libre

qui, voyant dans les métiers d'art l'expression du ravissement et de la sensualité du contact avec la matière, en vient à redouter ceux-ci et à leur prêter des attributs féminins. C'est du moins le propos qui semble relier ces divers écrits et leur donner un sens.

As a curator, I originally came to crafts as products, objects, things, and as an anthropologist, I came to things as containers of cultural meaning. Some ten years ago that all began to change after a moment of revelation at a Christmas show in Tam Irving's pottery in Vancouver.[1] As was my wont, I had made a preliminary selection of pieces for their sculptural and display qualities. But Tam's pieces demand more than looking at, and suddenly I was crying. The moment of epiphany was my realization that to use Tam's work properly, I would have to change my life. Instead of, or in addition to, pots for looking, Tam's are pots for cooking, for serving, for guests.

Shortly thereafter, I began the practice of *Chanoyu,* the Japanese tea ritual, with the intention, I thought at the time, of deepening my vocation as curator by learning to appreciate objects from within another cultural context. The respectful handling and viewing of objects in a tea demonstration had impressed me in ways I could not at the time articulate. I also intended to use my new knowledge to make a collection of tea wares for the Museum of Anthropology. *Chanoyu,* as I soon learned, is a complex, synchronized, and intimate ballet between host and guests that includes the cooking and serving of a multi-course meal as well the preparation and serving of thick and thin tea. That moment in Tam's pottery had, I realized, led me to the most refined expression of human sociability that I could find.

Chanoyu is also *Chado,* the Zen Way of Tea, and my interest in crafts as objects changed through the practice of Tea into an interest in craft as a self-transformative process.

Introduction[2]

From where we stand, on the edge of the twenty-first century, when realities are becoming virtual, texts are replacing action, and bodies are signs, to think "craft" is an act of either a radical or a sentimental consciousness. Both were present in the symposium. It was also so at the end of the last century, and I prepared myself to write this paper by reading some William Morris. For almost two decades, from 1877 until his death in 1896, Morris lectured

---

1 I will always be grateful to Glenn Allison for introducing me to ceramics and, particularly, for taking me to Irving's pottery that December.

2 Many of the ideas expressed in this paper originally occurred in conversations with Doris Shadbolt, whose commitment to crafts and crafting is inspirational.

on the relation of the medieval maker to his (sic) work. "And I will assert without fear of contradiction," he writes (quoted in Grennan 1945, 71), "that no human ingenuity can produce such work without pleasure being a third party to the brain that conceived it and the hand that fashioned it." He also writes of the craftsman in "The Aims of Art" (quoted in Grennan 1945, 71), "Poor devil, his work was of so little value that he was allowed to waste it by the hour in pleasing himself – and others." Morris's themes of pleasure in the work and of its trivialization still echo today, but now we understand that they are the two sides of the same coin in a patriarchal culture that fears and feminizes the crafts as expressions of the delight and sensuality of work- ing with the material world. This, at least, is the argument that seemed to link and make sense of this diverse set of papers.

The Papers

Margaret Visser opened our deliberations by arguing that there is still a "substantial interest" in craft, and then reduced this interest to a personal, playful, ecologically correct, and tasteful consumerism. And she is correct, of course, for as long as craft and art are discussed in terms of some variant on the binary opposition that art is to contemplation as craft is to usefulness, all we can do with the crafts is to learn to use them in a more or less cor- rect and witty way.

But other papers were presented that suggest that the way craft is talked and written about is changing and, maybe, just maybe, our ability to think, write, show, valorize, make, and craft the material world might be moving into a new paradigm, one that requires, establishes, and demands a separa- tion from the abstract language of art criticism.

Paul Mathieu asked the crucial question: "Why is it so seemingly easy to write about art and so difficult to do so about crafts?" He gave part of the answer, which is that craft does not let itself be easily deconstructed by con- temporary theory. Neil Forrest asked the question in a different way: "Are we hoping not to be confused with the fine arts, or be considered their hand- maiden?" (Notice the feminization of craft here.) Forrest's position that "craft must reassert its uniqueness, undertake new ventures and rethink its pedagogy to survive and flourish" also ran as a subtext through many of the papers.

The contradiction inherent in being the handmaiden of art was revealed in John Vollmer's paper. He began by asserting that fibre objects are the exception to his dismal observation that museum visitors are, except for their experiences in cafés, shops, or washrooms, "confused, disappointed, and bored." His reason is that fibre objects generate narratives or story making, which he illustrates with visitors' comments about an embroidered quilt from the 1860s. Fine. When, however, he jumps to contemporary production of fibre objects made "for the sake of making" – i.e., art – he leaves behind the popular production of narrative by non-specialist viewers and generates his own narrative of pure artspeak. Typical of this approach is his presentation of a wall hanging by Sarah Quinton, which is "based on basketry traditions, with specific reference to Japanese armour-making techniques":

> The maker's marks are complex and repetitive, setting up a rigorously controlled polyphony of theme and counterpoint. The artist's juxtaposition of hard and soft surfaces (wood moulding and waxed lacing tapes) literally builds a framework onto which a discourse about other contrasts can be projected. The viewer is asked to become enmeshed in a narrative that can only be characterized as polemic.

Clearly empathic with the makers of whom he writes, Vollmer's paper also disclosed another major theme of the conference: the professionalization of craft. Sandra Flood says it directly in her paper about the building of craft collections in British museums: "It appears that what is being recorded is the professionalization of craft due in part to the huge increase in the number of graduates from art colleges since the 1960s, graduates who train with painters and sculptors and want for themselves what the fine-art world offers in economic rewards and prestige, and who have in common, modernist discourses." Hence, Vollmer's adoption of the discourse of painting in order to validate the fabric artist.

Is there no other way? Is being "in the discourse," that is, accepting and reproducing the abstract, cerebral language of the academy, not to sell out the uniqueness of craft? Mathieu quotes Doris Shadbolt (1992) in a statement that calls for a reaffirmation of the distinction between craft and art: "Craft is about the very qualities that current art (theory) denies ...The theory-dominated cerebral climate which dominates today's art will change sooner or later, and then there will be a powerful reactive response. And a reaffirmation of the importance of the crafts will be at the centre of that response." But only, I will argue, if we have a language other than artspeak with which to make that affirmation.

Although few of the thousands of Japanese women who attend the silk-weaving workshops described by Millie Creighton will go on to become weavers, they are an educated audience for the professional "performers" of the tradition. For the professionals, writes Creighton, "the perpetuation of the craft performance would mean little if the modern Japanese audience, or at least some members of it, were not trained to appreciate the finer qualities of the craft performance." This is what Canadian curators and producers miss in the uncritical assumption either that the works speak for themselves, which they patently don't, or that we must artspeak for them, which, I maintain, crucially misrepresents them. But what would "craftspeak" or a discourse suitable to the distinction that craft is be like?

The need for a discourse specific to craft, which has "not defined its own theories of aesthetics," led Diane Sullivan to the language of the Pattern and Decoration movement in painting. Her discussion of the ego-denying nature of pattern was especially powerful, and I will return to this later. When, however, she refers to Amy Goldin's proclamation that, while "decoration may be intellectually empty, it need not be stupid," Sullivan, perhaps unintentionally, evoked for me the puritanical and patriarchal mindset that fears the sensuality of craft. Even if the post-modern movement's receptivity to decoration proves to be lasting, craft as a decorative art is still minor and feminized, as she acknowledged in her paper.

The Goldin quotation reminded me of Sir Ernest Gombrich's (1984) observation that throughout the Western tradition there have been periods when decoration and ornamentation were condemned not only as wasteful and indulgent, but as offences against reason. "If we follow the explicit formulation of this ambivalence towards decoration to its source," he writes (1984, 18), "we are led from the criticism of art to that of speech." For it was in the ancient schools of oratory that the issue was first articulated and debated. According to Plato, Socrates urged his students to be on guard against the seduction of fine speech. In the history of Greek rhetorical theory, purists, called Atticists, developed an aesthetic of prejudice against "the artifice of so-called Asiatic oratory with its rhythmic cadences and its far fetched imagery" (p. 10). They developed a "cult of the plain and simple," which was commended as follows by the Roman orator Cicero:

> For just as some women are said to be more beautiful when unadorned, because this suits them, so this plain style delights, even though it lacks embellishments. In such a case every conspicuous ornament, the pearls, as it were, will be removed, no curling iron will be applied, cosmetic, white and rouge, will be rejected, all that remains will be neatness and cleanliness. The language will be pure and Latin, limpid and straight, always aiming first at propriety. (Quoted in Gombrich 1984, 19)

In other words, what is spurned by Cicero and other purists in the academy, then as now, is the feminine. I will return to this later.

Just as William Morris turned to the Middle Ages to fuel his critique of his own time, anthropologists in our time turn to the Other.

A few years ago (Halpin 1989), I listed the materials out of which the First Nations objects in the Glenbow's much-publicized exhibition *The Spirit Sings* were made, and made in large part by women. Notice the relationship to matter and the material world that it evokes: birchbark, spruce root, metal nails, resin caulking, plant-fibre cordage, porcupine quills, caribou hides, sinew, red ochre, guillemot claws, bone, organic dyes, intestines, caribou long-bones, animal teeth, walrus ivory, wool, silk-brocade ribbons, silk thread, glass beads, cotton thread, silver, metal beads, mink skins, horsehair, velvet, brass beads, sateen, copper, sequins, paper, cardboard, metal hooks and eyes, tinsel braid, moose hair, aniline dyes, metal buttons, ash-splints, sweetgrass, waxed twine, argillite, beaver dewclaws, cherry bark, metal cones, animal hair, glass, clay, limestone, antler, shell beads, cheese-cloth, wire, paint, deerskin, wild-duck skin, eagle feathers, metal staples, stroud, cattail reeds, sandstone, elk skin, weasel fur, hackle feathers, antelope skin, human hair, brass tacks, elk horn, deer hooves, bear claws, buffalo horn, canvas, bird quills, otter fur, native copper, mountain-sheep horn, eleagnus seeds, dentalia, bird bone, babiche, plastic beads, sealskin, loon's beak, wolf fur, wolverine fur, caribou fur, reindeer fur, ivory, nephrite, quartz, whalebone, maidenhair fern, surf grass, bear grass, mountain-goat wool, nettle fibre, sea-otter fur, puffin beaks, mountain-goat horn, abalone shell, iron, haliotis shell, mica, flicker feathers, sea-otter teeth, graphite, basalt, opercula, whale baleen, and various kinds of wood.

What this list reveals is a profound knowledge of materials, of the properties of matter, sensuously acquired. The great MIT scientist, Cyril Stanley Smith (1981, 123), writes that, beginning in the 1930s, materials scientists forsook their own "partially intuitive knowledge of materials to worship at the shrine of mathematics, a trend reinforced by the curious human tendency to laud the more abstract." Elsewhere (1981, 367), he writes, "Science in the past has been almost synonymous with the distrust of the senses," a tendency that finds its ultimate expression in the simplicity of the subatomic world, that is, science as the exercise of pure thought. Note that he is writing of the past, for Smith (1981, viii) himself was a new kind of materials scientist who "had been studying the history of metals for many years before [he] finally realized that the best sources for the early period were not the conventional written documents of the historian but the material artifacts in art museums." Carol Mayer's paper about teaching craft students at the Museum of Anthropology celebrates that same wisdom and, I think, provides the answer to Forrest's call for a rethinking of the pedagogy of craft. Augment or, more radically, replace, instruction in the academy, where craft students will be forever handmaidens to the fine arts, by introducing them, as Mayer did, to their own illustrious ancestors, the great materials specialists of the past in the museum.

This is frequently done in British Columbia, where First Nations makers have special access to the works of their ancestors in museums, and are often given space and other resources for their work. At the Museum of Anthropology we have just set aside funds for First Nations residencies (supported by the sales of First Nations works in the museum anthropology shop) to regularize the arrangement. One thing that happens, and will undoubtedly happen to students of the crafts from other traditions, is that First Nations artists now show and sell in two very different settings: those who follow their ancestral traditions show in museums (these are called craftsmen and women by the others), and those who are trained in the academy show in art galleries. The exceptions, such as the traditionalist Haida artist Robert Davidson, who recently had a show at the Vancouver Art Gallery, are so rare as to prove the point. Both groups continually innovate, but it takes knowledge of the culture to recognize the innovations by the traditionalists.

As a craftsperson in the university, Michele Hardy discovered that her way of knowing, with her whole body, was devalued and marginalized. One of the recurrent themes in many of the papers presented here were challenges to what Hardy terms "the authority science has assumed over knowledge." While Hardy found a way of understanding her marginalization as a woman and a craftsperson in feminist theory, she stops short of saying, as I have and Diane Sullivan did, that craft itself is feminized by the academy.

This is, I think, clearly revealed in Virginia Wright's paper on the history of craft education, where "real" design after the war "was seen to be the territory of the boys with the toys." Her history of the devaluation of crafts and their assignment to academic limbo, where she asserts they remain today, is challenged by Jacques Giard and Neil Forrest and by Diane Sullivan's hopeful claims of a post-modern receptivity to craft values and traditions.

Mathieu's use of the thought of Michel Foucault – especially the notions of utopia (unreal spaces) and heterotopia (other spaces) – permits us to expand the restricted and cramped little space of craft to which Margaret Visser consigned it in her keynote address to larger and more heroic dimensions. I especially like the Foucauldian comparison of utopias, representational, and visual art with heterotopias, presentational pottery, and participation in life. "This is why," says Mathieu, quoting Foucault, "utopias permit fables and discourses, they run with the very grain of language and are part of the very dimension of *fabula;* heterotopias... dessicate speech, stop words in their tracks, contest the very possibility of language at its source; they dissolve our myths and sterilize the lyricism of our sentences."

And here we reach the heart of the matter, which is that craft dissolves language because it originally preceded it; it gives it no place to anchor. Although Michel Paradis's French is a bit beyond my poor skill in the language,[3] if I grasp his research, it adds to the traditional discourse of semiotics (the science of signs) the resistance of matter to the shaping hand and tool and thereby the "accidental" production of meaningful signs. By introducing semiotics into the symposium, he gives me licence, I hope you might agree, to augment his discussion with the thought of another French semiotician, Julia Kristeva.

Kristeva, professor of linguistics and a practising psychoanalyst in Paris, is a theorist of the role of language in the constitution and productions of the "speaking subject." Her work permits us to examine the relations between the rhythmic and symbolic, the body and the mind, which is what I think characterizes craft and distinguishes it from post-Renaissance art.

Most pertinent to this paper is Kristeva's postulation of the semiotic as the *materiality* of language, its rhythms, its poetry, that which both lies outside the symbolic order and is disruptive of it. "It was perhaps also necessary to be a *woman,*" she writes (1980, x), "to attempt to take up that exorbitant wager of carrying the rational project to the outer borders of the signifying venture of men." Central to her theory is that there is a dialectical relation between the semiotic and symbolic functions in language. The French language can shift the meaning of an abstract noun to its concrete counterpart by changing the gender. Thus, *la sémiotique* is "semiotics," the science of signs (cf. Roland Barthes, Thomas Sebeok, Umberto Eco, and Michel Paradis). Kristeva's *le sémiotique,* on the other hand, refers to the body's phys-

3 I thank Doris Shadbolt for helping me translate this paper.

iological drives and rhythms and how these show up in language or constitute a poetry of the body in language (Roudiez 1980, 17-18). The symbolic is a domain of representation, position, judgement, grammatical and social restraints – of ego, in short. Kristeva's semiotic, on the other hand, is non-representational, non-egoistic. John Lechte (1990, 129), Kristeva's student and intellectual biographer, writes that her semiotic is about "the voice as rhythm and timbre, the body as movement, gesture, and rhythm. Prosody, word-plays, and especially laughter fall within the ambit of the semiotic."

At the foundation of all psychoanalytic theory is the notion of an unconscious, unknown to the ego, that nonetheless expresses itself in speech and symptoms. The work of the psychoanalyst is to listen to it. It speaks. More precisely, for Kristeva, it speaks through a shattering of the wall of repression and judgement; it speaks, for Lechte (1990, 37), between the lines. "Could it be, then," he asks, "that the unconscious only becomes manifest in the performance?" This is the question I am trying to answer, the question whose answer, I think, could point the way to an appropriate discourse for craft. How does the unconscious speak in the skill of the maker? How does the unconscious speak in the work of craft?

Conclusion

In this concluding section, I parallel Neil Forrest's discussion of craft, ritual, and architecture in the Western tradition by drawing on my own knowledge of Japanese practices. In the Japanese Way of Tea, the Kabuki and Noh Theatres, the Way of the Sword, the Way of Archery, calligraphy, gardens, ceramics, and the martial arts, gestural practice is broken down into its constituent forms, and these are repeated in ever longer sequences until they become habituated or sedimented in the body below the level of consciousness awareness (Zarelli 1990, 133-34). "When skill reaches a certain level," writes the musician Stephen Nachmanovitch (1990, 74), "it hides itself." The practitioner is thereby freed from consciousness "about" technique to a state of consciousness "through" technique. This is a state of concentratedness, of a focusing of mind and body, that can lead to peak experiences, as well as extraordinary gestural performance.

In *Art as Experience* (1980 [1934], 264), John Dewey writes about the sedimentations of habitual action as constituting "a part of the self,... a modification [that] extends beyond acquisition of greater facility and skill." But this extended self is not an ego, for habits are anonymous or, in Dewey's term, "pre-objective." Unlike the fragmented and de-stabilized ego of post-modernism, Dewey's habituated self is a stable one. It is this self, trained beyond or beneath the opportunings of the ego, that crafting adds to the human being.

In the Japanese traditions, the cultivation of skill through the repetition of forms marks the highest achievements of which humans are capable and, when intention and striving are neutralized, lead to the possibility of attaining *satori,* or enlightenment. Humans are incarnate beings, and the crafting and transforming of our environments are also acts of self-cultivation and self-transformation (see Kondo 1990). Every skilled practitioner of a craft knows this already. That is why they do it.

Postscript

It wasn't until after I returned from the conference that I discovered Alberto Manguel's and Robert Enright's papers from a symposium on museum publishing held in Calgary in 1992. Their session was called "Stamping out Artspeak," and they made the argument that I attempted above, with good-humoured John Vollmer as my example, with more eloquence and far more deserving examples than I did; I cite their articles below for the interested reader.

References

Dewey, John. 1980 [1934]. *Art as Experience.* New York: Putnam.

Enright, Robert. 1993. "Blueline for the Future, Redline for the Present: A Critical Autobiography," *Muse* 10, no. 4:30-32.

Grennan, Margaret R. 1945. *William Morris: Medievalist and Revolutionary.* New York: Russell & Russell.

Gombrich, E.H. 1984. *The Sense of Order: A Study in the Psychology of Decorative Art.* 2nd ed. Ithaca, N.Y.: Cornell University Press.

Grosz, Elizabeth. 1989. *Sexual Subversions: Three French Feminists.* Sydney, Australia: Allen & Unwin.

Halpin, Marjorie. 1989. "The Spirit Sings." *Culture* 8, no. 1: 89-93.

Kondo, Dorinne E. 1990. *Crafting Selves: Power, Gender and Discourses of Identity in a Japanese Workplace.* Chicago: University of Chicago Press.

Kristeva, Julia. 1980. "The Ethics of Linguistics." In *Desire in Language,* ed. by Leon S. Roudiez. trans. by Th. Gora, A. Jardine, and L.S., Roudiez, 23-35. New York: Columbia University Press.

– – – 1989. *Black Sun: Depression and Melancholia.* Trans. by Leon S. Roudiez. New York: Columbia University Press.

Lechte, John. 1990. *Julia Kristeva*. London: Routledge.

Manguel, Alberto. 1993. "Stamping out Artspeak," *Muse* 10, no. 4: 27-29.

Nachmanovitch, Stephen. 1990. *Free Play: The Power of Imagination in Life and the Arts*. Los Angeles: Jeremy P. Tarcher.

Roudiez, Leon S. 1980. Introduction in Julia Kristeva, *Desire in Language,* 1-20.

Shadbolt, Doris. 1992. *Leadline Magazine* (published by Artists in Stained Glass, Toronto), 5.

Smith, Cyril Stanley. 1981. *A Search for Structure: Selected Essays on Science, Art, and History*. Cambridge, Mass.: M.I.T Press.

Zarelli, Phillip. 1990. "What Does It Mean to 'Become the Character': Power, Presence, and Transcendence." In *Intercultural Studies of Theatre and Ritual,* Richard Schechner and Willa Appel, eds., 131-48. Cambridge: Harvard University Press.